THE POWER OF PR

EFFECTIVELY GROW AND SCALE YOUR BUSINESS THROUGH STRATEGIC STORYTELLING

NICOLA J ROWLEY

AND CO.

DEDICATION

This book is dedicated to all our wonderful clients, past and present, who have entrusted NJRPR with telling their stories...

CONTENTS

Introduction   7
My Story   15

1. PR BASICS   21
   What is PR?   21
   How can PR help you?   23
   How PR can't help you...   24
   Your why...   26

2. THE PR STORYTELLING FRAMEWORK™   32
   What it is and how it can help you   32

3. WHAT NEEDS TO BE IN PLACE   37
   Your Story   38
   Search Engine Optimisation (SEO)   40
   Professional Images   41
   Your Biography   45
   Ideal Clients   48

4. GETTING STRATEGIC   53
   Key Messages   53
   Business Objectives   54
   Communications Objectives   57

5. STORYTELLING, NOT SELLING   70
   How to deeper connect with your audience   75
   The angles of your story exercise   78

6. FACING THE FEAR   82
   Working on your self belief, confidence and   84
   gaining clarity
   It's always about them and not you   87

7. APPROACHING JOURNALISTS 90
   What journalists want 97
   What journalists don't want 97
   The power of an opinion piece 99
   Consistency 102
   What to say, what to do and how often 103

8. WHAT TO DO IN A CRISIS 106
   Inaccuracies and what to do about them 109
   The importance of a crisis Q&A document 114
   Being misquoted 117

9. MAKING A CAMPAIGN SUCCESSFUL 119
   What works and why 119
   Press releases 125

10. NOW WHAT? 133
   In Conclusion... 146

   In their own words... 153
   About the Author 157
   Ways you can work with Nicola J Rowley from NJRPR... 159

INTRODUCTION

When I first started thinking about writing a book around PR and strategic storytelling, even though I've worked in the media for over 25 years, I thought, how could I make it an interesting read and a book that you would want to keep coming back to?

As a small business owner, you may or may not have some idea of how PR can help you. But all too often, those working in the industry intrinsically see it as a marketing tool to raise awareness for brands, products, or personalities, without looking at the bigger picture and wider impact that PR can have on others.

I know this is a sweeping statement and there are so many things that PR can help with, alongside media relations including reputation management, internal communications, community relations, Public Affairs and online and social media management.

But for the purpose of this book, I'd like to focus on how strategic storytelling can help entrepreneurs like you effectively grow and scale your business, as I believe it's the most powerful marketing tool you have.

Ever since I was six, and wrote my first story about a cat, a witch, and a spaceship, nothing lights me up in the way that writing, and storytelling do. It's why I trained and worked as a journalist in various newsrooms across the UK and internationally for thirteen years before I even considered a career in PR. When I was thinking about making that change, I remember having a conversation with one of my best friends, saying I thought I should work in charity PR. The reason? I'm all about helping others.

But with a background in news and as BBC Three's Entertainment Reporter, having never written a press release before, I found it easier to get my foot in the door of a specialist entertainment PR agency. That sense of wanting to help others never left me, though, and when I started my own Communications Agency (NJRPR) in March 2019, I realised how PR is a perfect vehicle to be able to do this.

From the outside, PR is viewed as a shallow choice of profession thanks in part to its depiction in the hugely successful TV show *Absolutely Fabulous*. It's seen as all swanky parties and jazz hands as you make a brand or product look as good as possible.

All I can tell you is that from the moment I started working as an Account Manager, moved my way up to Associate Director level in various agencies and then looked after launches, stunts and publicity in-house for big brands, I've been about as far removed from a 'typical PR' as you can get.

I care much more about the person behind the story, the experience they have gone through, and the way they have reached where they are, than anything else. There are journalists too, who are just hungry for stories. So much so, that they forget there are real people behind the headlines. They forget that their experiences have been difficult and, at times, might have even broken them. I give those journalists a wide berth because it's too important to me that any client of mine is looked after and guided through what can feel like a very scary process to get visible.

If you're reading this as a small business owner and you're still going through a life-defining experience, please know that PR isn't a way to piece yourself back together again. And it's usually best to talk from the scar rather than the wound (i.e., when you're ready to do so). But it can enable you to share your story with others so, if they're also experiencing a problem, they know there is hope and light at the end of the tunnel. Some of the most inspirational women I work with have done this and continue to do this today. Their stories are woven throughout this book to provide a source of inspiration for you.

So yes, there are many who work in PR who focus just on helping build awareness for their clients and in turn, help to feed their egos and potentially drive sales through media coverage. But I don't believe that's what PR should be about.

Journalists often describe PR as the dark side. It's the moment you cross the line from impartiality and storytelling and are effectively selling things to people. But if you tell your story in an authentic, real, and honest way, the impact you're able to have through the media and beyond is profound. Please never underestimate how important sharing your story could be to someone else. Never underestimate the difference that it could make to their lives.

The other thing that business owners tend to do is focus solely on securing media coverage, thinking this is the magic formula that will secure them the credibility and expert status that they crave. But equally, having your own podcast, writing guest blogs and posts, carefully crafted opinion pieces, speaking on stages and at events, and marrying any PR activity with an integrated social media strategy, all helps you to reach a larger audience in an engaging way.

Perhaps you're a hypnotherapist who helps heal trauma, or a nutritionist who can help people get back on the straight and narrow with their diet or understand why they're suffering so much with indigestive pain. Maybe you specialise in helping others declutter their lives, giving them that sense of freedom that they've never had, or you're a mindset coach, who helps them to look at their current situation in a completely different way.

You may have a product-based business and the items you sell quite literally spread happiness, or perhaps it's a business where you're looking to evoke more emotion or education through books, candles, or t-shirts with empowering slogans.

Whatever you do as a small business owner, you have the power to transform lives, and that power comes from sharing your story and telling people the journey that you have been on to get to where you are. You might be right at the start of that journey. You might well be still struggling with being in debt. But you could also be that person who has been in debt and is now running a hugely successful business. And it's those kinds of stories that the media and other platforms could be interested in.

Perhaps you have done something that no one else has done before. Maybe you're seventy and last week you completed a tandem skydive and raised thousands of pounds for charity. Perhaps you run a support group for women over the age of forty-five and want to show them that life is for living and to not give up. Maybe you work from a unique office space like a caravan on your driveway at home, or you work from a tree house at the bottom of the garden. Whatever it is, these are the kind of things that will resonate with people.

Stories and storytelling are so important because they allow us to get under the skin to really understand where you're coming from. They provide an emotional connection between you and your audience. All too often though, we hold back from telling them because we're worried about what others might think, or what they might say, and we use this as an excuse to stay hidden.

But whilst it is very much your story, and you should only share the parts of it that you're happy to, you have to remember it's not about you. I know that sounds a funny thing to say, but please bear with me.

As a business owner, you have a gift. Now you need to go out there and share that gift, telling people what it is you do, and how you can help them. In doing this, your story, amplified through the power of PR, will enable you to connect with more people on a deeper level. You will resonate with your ideal clients because they will understand not only what you do, but the journey you have been on to get to where you are.

So, when it came to writing this book, I wanted to provide you with a way to understand the steps to take so PR can be used as part of your marketing toolkit. Not only does it cement your expert status, add to your credibility and reach, but it's the impact you can have on other people's lives, your ideal clients, which is beyond important.

So now it's time for you to step up and step out like never before. No more hiding and no more saying, 'What if...' or, 'I'll just wait until I get everything aligned before I go out there and let people know what I do.'

They need to hear you now.

Maybe it's a single mum who is struggling because her child has developed an unfortunate speech impediment and you're an independent speech therapist. Maybe it's a lady who is in agonising back pain because she's been working from home for too long and you're an osteopath.

You need to be telling people how they can find you, and where you are. But more than that, they need to know that you're the person who can help with the transformation they crave – not someone else who also does what you do.

Because no one else is you and that is your superpower.

You are unique in the way that you can help them.

And only you have been on the journey that you have, to get to where you are.

Those experiences you have gone through – they are part and parcel of that journey. They will help someone to understand and resonate with you, and in turn, they will want to work with you.

Always think of PR as a trail of breadcrumbs that can help someone reach their destination and solve their problem.

Used correctly, PR can be impactful, and it can change lives.

Let's not look at it as just an awareness raising tool to make subsequent sales or a way to shout through a loud hailer saying, 'Look at me!'

There's much more to it than that.

PR is the element of the marketing mix that can show people that you care. And that's why sharing your story and owning your story is so important.

As you go through this book, you will see there's much more to PR than just securing media by approaching the first journalist or publication you think of and telling them everything. PR needs to be approached in a strategic way, crafted so that it also works for you, and it enables you to help your clients at the same time.

Are you ready? If so, let's begin to grow and scale your business through strategic storytelling, using the undeniable power of PR.

Nicola J Rowley, Founder NJRPR – January 2022

MY STORY

The first thing I'd like you to know about me is that I will never ask you to do something that I haven't already done myself. I'm a firm believer in walking the walk and talking the talk.

When I say it's important to tell your story, it wouldn't make sense if I didn't tell you mine.

So here it is. This, of course, is not all my story, but it's where I believe it begins in terms of my transformation from rock bottom to where I am now.

It begins when I was forty and had just returned to work after a year's maternity leave – struggling with severe separation anxiety. Up until the arrival of our son J, I think it's fair to say that whilst I was ambitious, I'd hit a glass ceiling in my career. I had also been guilty of allowing life to just pass me by…

* * *

It was a dark and windy evening in early October 2015. I looked at the series of red taillights stretching out in front of me on the A3 and my heart sank. It was obvious, no matter how much I wanted to, I was going nowhere fast. And yet again, I was going to be late. I managed to take a couple of deep breaths before I dialled the number for the nursery. It was the second such call I'd had to make that week. Thankfully, the voice on the end of the phone seemed suitably understanding. Perhaps they could sense my anguish. Either way, I tried to stay calm as I explained I would be arriving after 6:30pm.

As soon as I pressed the button to disconnect the call, tears began to prick my eyes. This wasn't what I thought being a mum should be like.

I'd returned to work a few weeks earlier, a few days a week at first and now I was back full-time, five days a week starting at 8:30am and finishing at 5pm. But factoring in the commute meant that I was only seeing my son for half an hour a day before the bath, milk, story bedtime routine that had become even more precious than before.

At that moment, I remember being consumed by a wave of loneliness. I felt completely lost and didn't know what to do.

I took a deep breath between sobs and glanced at the cars, also stationary, in the lanes on either side. I wondered whether anyone else felt the same way or had I, in some way, brought this on myself?

Finally, when I arrived at the nursery, my son was bundled into his car seat whilst I gathered his things from inside. It was so late that I went home that night not knowing what kind of a day he'd had. And as he was only just one, he couldn't tell me either.

That night, after he was settled and asleep, I sat down and cried.

Something inside me literally broke. I was broken and I knew I couldn't carry on this way, but I felt I had no choice. We had bills to pay, and with both of us working full-time to make ends meet, I couldn't see a way around the situation I now found myself in. I felt like I didn't have a choice.

Being a mum was everything I'd hoped it would be and more besides. But I was missing those all-important precious moments; moments I knew I would never get back again.

I couldn't get away from the fact that someone else was bringing up my little boy during the day and it ate away at me like nothing else had done before.

There's no doubt about it, separation anxiety is a scary and incredibly debilitating condition. I'd struggled since the day after J was born when he'd been rushed up to the neo-natal intensive care unit at St Peter's Hospital in Chertsey. That moment when his blood sugar levels had plummeted dangerously low and he was hooked up to every conceivable machine, being fed my milk offerings through a tube in his nose.

We'd stared helplessly as he'd had to wear newborn socks on his tiny hands to prevent him from pulling out the tubes connected to his veins that were helping to keep him alive.

For me, the anxiety set in after I'd woken in the middle of the night in the sterile surroundings of the hospital and stared at the empty cot next to my bed.

Carrying a baby, who you talk to, sing to, and feel inside of you for nine months – to no longer have them with you, is nothing short of devastating.

I knew of course, I could see him whenever I wanted to, and frequently, I was the only one wandering the empty hospital corridors at 2am, having just watched him sleeping soundly in his plastic crib. But every time I made the walk, and in the beginning, it was just a waddle, post C-section, I had to pass all the other mums, catch sight of them cradling their babies lovingly and hear the familiar cries of the newborns as they settled back to sleep.

And now, after spending the last twelve months joined at the hip doing everything together, the separation anxiety was back with a vengeance. It ate away at me like never before. Every moment of every day. Somewhere along the way I had lost my identity and had immersed myself so wholly in being a mum, that I could no longer see a way past it.

I'd been to see my doctor and he'd tried to understand my reluctance to return to work. In the end, his solution was to send me to a psychiatrist, who 'might be able to help.'

He didn't. The meeting with said psychiatrist felt strange. There I was, sat in front of a middle-aged, balding man who asked lots of probing questions. How was my childhood? Had anything traumatic ever happened to me? My answers just served to remind me of what I already knew – I was perfectly sane; I just didn't want to be apart from my son.

The psychiatrist's assessment arrived in the post two weeks later. He was confused and couldn't understand why I was so 'stressed out' at the prospect of only seeing my child for thirty minutes a day. Take anti-depressants, he suggested, as if that would fix everything. Knowing that wasn't the solution, I ignored him and his diagnosis.

Something else happened on that journey on the A3 which also served to highlight the situation I was in. Whilst I was still stationary and going nowhere fast, my mobile beeped to signal I had a new message. I gave it a cursory glance and saw it was from one of the girls from my NCT group asking about meeting up for what would have been the regular Wednesday get together. I didn't read the rest of the message – I didn't need to.

It highlighted how isolated I felt. I didn't have a community of other mums around me. I was the one doing the daily grind, trying to juggle family and work life, and barely keeping up with everything, whilst some of them could afford to stay at home or run their own businesses so they had more flexibility to continue meeting up.

And that's why that journey on the A3 became the defining moment. That night, I decided to swim instead of sink; something had to change. At this point, I didn't know any of the answers. I knew I wanted to be a children's author and I knew a lot about PR and the media, but I had no idea how to scale anything or even get a book published, let alone attract enough of the right clients so I could have the freedom I craved so much. Most of all, at the heart of everything, I wanted to be there for my son.

So, from that moment on I became laser focused. If this was what I truly wanted, then I had to find a way to be able to make this happen. Whatever it would take, I knew I could become the kind of mum I always dreamt I would be.

I became intentional about what I wanted. I knew for me the most important thing was to be the mum at the school gates doing both the drop-offs and pick-ups. I had a goal and now, somehow, I had to make it a reality.

With each new job I applied for, I kept this in mind. I was only interested in maternity cover contracts – for my own sanity initially, I needed to know there was an end in sight. Then I negotiated flexible hours and a way of working that helped me.

I hadn't intended to continue much beyond that first contract, but sometimes, when opportunities present themselves and they're too good to be true, you just have to go with them. And so, I began working in a senior full-time role, condensed into a four-day week. I absolutely loved my job and everything that went with it – even the early starts and late finishes. But more importantly, it was a twenty-five-minute drive from home, and I was able to spend Fridays with my son.

As he was born in August, J has always been one of the youngest in his class. So, as much as I loved the role I was in, I also knew the goal of being mum on the school gate was looming and I would only be able to stay for a year. After that, it was down to me to find a way to navigate everything and make the finances make sense.

Thankfully, by this time I had a brilliant business coach, who made me realise the importance of laser-focused goal setting.

My story is far from complete and as I write this, I have set up my own Communications Agency, helping female entrepreneurs with strategic PR storytelling and working with brands in the leisure and entertainment industries, and of course writing books; children's books, but also this one for each and every one of you.

I don't have all the answers, but I have worked out a lot of things. And yes, for that first all-important year whilst J was in Reception, I was the mum on the school gates – just as I always wanted to be.

1

PR BASICS

WHAT IS PR?

A s a business owner, when thinking about PR for the first time, it can feel daunting and overwhelming. Where do you start? What do you need to do to be successful? And how can you replicate some of the success you may see your peers getting?

My greatest piece of advice when it comes to PR is to stay in your own lane and concentrate on you and your brand. Don't be swayed by shiny object syndrome – the latest fad that you must be a part of. Instead, get to know your ideal client, their likes, dislikes, where they spend time together and where they get their news. These are all fundamental pieces of the PR puzzle that, when put together, will help you create the picture you have been working towards.

I trained as a journalist and worked in various newsrooms in the UK and internationally for thirteen years before I even entertained crossing to 'the dark side'. PR has always been considered in journalist circles to be the easier option of career. No more having to find your story, ensuring you work to tight deadlines to file it, or in my case, presenting it either on the radio in news bulletins or evening news shows, or through reports for television. But there was always a part of me that was curious about PR. Having worked in national news for several years, it felt like I was where I'd always wanted to be. But something was missing. I couldn't see myself standing on a red carpet in the freezing cold, interviewing celebrities about their latest projects when I turned fifty. I also wanted a career that meant I could be more creative. So, I started to explore my options. It all started one late shift at the BBC News Channel, when I saw an advert for a PR Manager for The Comedy Club. I didn't apply, but something made me think there was more to PR than met the eye. The advert made it sound like it would be so much fun.

Fast forward a few years and I decided to see if it was indeed possible to take voluntary redundancy and start a whole new career at the same time. I left the BBC on a Friday afternoon in May 2008 and started my new chapter at an entertainment focused PR agency on the Monday. Up until this point, I'd never written a press release. I didn't know anything about PR, aside from the fact that I'd loved the job application process I'd just been through to secure my role as an Account Manager. I also loved the energy of the agency and one of the co-founders had a lot of faith in me.

Being the sort of person that likes to have qualifications to back things up, I also enrolled in a CIM accredited Marketing Communications Diploma, which I worked on in parallel to my new job. I condensed my learning into twelve months instead of the recommended two years, studying evenings after long hours at work. On the course, I realised there are many textbook definitions of PR, and I could quite happily quote them for you, but the following is the analogy that I think makes it easiest to understand:

> *"If a young man tells his date how handsome, smart and successful he is – that's advertising. If the young man tells his date she's intelligent, looks lovely, and is a great conversationalist, he's saying the right things to the right person and that's marketing. If someone else tells the young woman how handsome, smart and successful her date is – that's PR."*

— S.H. SIMMONS

In essence, PR is that all-important third-party endorsement of your product, business or what you do. It is infinitely more valuable because that opinion comes via a journalist, editor or another valuable third-party. It helps to highlight your expertise and adds to your credibility. Rather than just relying on your ideal client to have seen or heard your contribution somewhere, by highlighting where you have been featured prominently on your website with an 'as featured in'... followed by the media logos, you are telling them you're an industry expert. In short, it helps set you apart. And who doesn't want to work with someone who really knows what they're doing and has been featured in the media, spoken on big stages, or been interviewed on key podcasts too?

HOW CAN PR HELP YOU?

Please don't think that PR is the be all and end all when it comes to your marketing. It should never be viewed in isolation and is very much part of the mix, but here are just some of the ways it can help:

- PR can strategically help raise your profile and that of your business.
- It can increase your credibility and lead more people to want to work with you.
- It can help cement your expert status and that of your brand.
- It can help you to reach your ideal clients through storytelling.
- It's a powerful third-party endorsement of what you do.
- PR can help raise your reach and impact.
- It can open new doors to other exciting opportunities / collaborations.

HOW PR CAN'T HELP YOU...

There have been so many times in my career when the success of a whole campaign has been placed firmly at the door of PR. But as I mentioned, it should never be seen in isolation when it comes to driving results. Yes, it's a cost-effective way to spread your message, but it also needs to be enhanced through other marketing activity. Here are a few ways that PR can't help you:

- It can't immediately make sales – though it can lead to an uplift in sales through awareness raising, this can and does usually take time. PR should always be approached strategically with a plan in place.
- There are never any guarantees about securing coverage.
- It can't solve all problems with your business.
- It is not a substitution for all other Marketing to reduce costs.
- It can't make something you want to talk about into front page news.

- It can't help you cover up something that's not right with your business or brand.

I realised early on in my PR career, that it was invaluable to have had those years of experience as a journalist. I inherently knew what made a good story; I knew how busy newsrooms worked and how to pitch to secure coverage, often and well. It helps that I'm a people person and love speaking to everyone, so picking up the phone and talking to journalists didn't faze me. I knew what they needed and how something could work for them (nowadays, I should mention that most journalists prefer to be contacted via email in the first instance).

Once you have read this book, I'm hoping that you too will understand what a powerful tool PR can be for your business – especially when you focus on strategic storytelling.

A great place to start when it comes to working out the elements of your story, is to understand why you began your business in the first place. Think about the following:

- What makes your business unique?
- Why should someone care about your story?

Then ask yourself:

- What is the reason you do what you do?
- And how has that all-important reason helped you to continue your journey?

As you will have seen from my story, my driving force for my business is the need to have flexibility so I can be there for my son. It's my non-negotiable. Now over to you...

YOUR WHY...

You may have heard people talking about their Why, but up until now not really understood what they meant. It's simple. Your Why is the one thing that will help motivate you when things get tough. It's your reason for keeping going. In short, it's your anchor that enables you to continue your journey as a business owner, no matter what. It's important that you identify yours at the start of your journey because you will keep coming back to it, time and again. In other words, it has an emotional pull on you like nothing else. Trust me, when things get difficult in your business, knowing what your Why is will help when you're faced with any struggles, and it will allow you to face them head on and still be able to power through.

Ever since my son J was born, I just wanted to be there for him. But alongside this, I've also wanted to not compromise who I am as a person. It's why I worked so hard to set up my own Communications Agency, to make it the success that it is today.

Once I'd made the decision to swim and not sink, my overall goal became being the mum I'd always wanted to be, so he knows I'm there for him, setting the best possible example that I can. My journey to reach this point has taken six years. But I began it by becoming intentional about getting to where I wanted to be and within what timeframe (more on that as we explore setting goals in Chapter Four).

As a business owner, you may have decided, like me, you needed more flexibility in your life than a nine-to-five job can give you. You might have made a promise to someone that you would do something and now you want to honour it. Whatever it is, there will be a reason why you get out of bed in the morning and work in and on your business.

At the end of the day though, your Why is just that. It's yours. It needs to be something that you simply must work towards, or it has such a pull on you, no matter what happens, you won't give up.

Before we go any further, I should mention it's worth making lots of notes as you go through the book. It's worth investing in a dedicated notepad so you can come back to each of the exercises, or at least make a note of where everything is. Scribble on the pages as you go along if it helps. I find turning over the corners and underlining/highlighting important sentences or paragraphs is always super helpful, and I'm a huge fan of post it notes. But please do it as you go along, otherwise you will spend ages trying to go back at the end and asking yourself, now where was that bit that said x, y, z?

So, now you have a pen and notebook, write down all the things that you think could have as strong an emotional pull on you as mine has had, and continues to have, on me.

Being there for J isn't an option for me – it's part and parcel of who I am, and I want him to grow up knowing that I've been around, and he can come to me whenever he needs me. But I also haven't wanted to compromise who I am – so it's been equally important that he sees me follow my dreams and live out my purpose in helping small business owners like you be able to tell their stories through strategic PR storytelling. It's important that J knows one day he too can follow his dreams and do something that will help impact the lives of others.

If you're being honest with yourself, and throughout this process it's important that you are, you have already known what your Why is for some time.

For some of you though, it might be there but require a bit more work for you to realise what motivates, inspires, or drives you forward no matter what.

This is the beauty of writing everything down. And your notes are just that – they're yours, so it's just like you're talking to yourself but working out exactly what you want in your life.

Now think about how you feel when you think about your Why. Does it make you sad or does it create an emotional response from you every time you think about it? If it does, great – this sounds like it really is your Why. If not, be careful and look back at your list again. Remember, it must pull at the heart strings even just a little bit to work effectively.

Initially when I worked mine out, it used to literally make me cry. But in fairness, that was because I was only seeing J for half an hour a day, Monday to Friday, and it was breaking me. Now my response to my Why is more of a dogged determination to make everything work no matter what – because it must. And absolutely nothing, not money, fear, procrastination, can hold me back from being there for him. Everything else follows from this.

The emotional response that you have to your Why is important because it will remind you how important this one thing is to you. It will ensure no matter how many wobbles you have, there is no choice but to keep going.

Now that you know what it is, write out your Why on a post it note or print it out on a piece of paper in big letters and have it somewhere you will see it every day. That way there is no escape from it. It should be one of the first things you see when you wake up in the morning and whilst your initial reaction might be, 'Urgh, I can't think about that right now,' without realising it, you're successfully programming your unconscious mind into taking it on board.

* * *

Business case study

Kate Hopewell-Smith Professional Photographer, Filmmaker & Trainer

Someone who knows only too well the importance of identifying their Why early on is Award-winning Sony European Ambassador, Kate Hopewell-Smith. Before she became a mum, Kate was working as an Account Director for an International Branding Agency in London, looking after high-profile clients. But when she went on maternity leave with her daughter, she was already pretty sure she wouldn't be returning, as she had plans to move out of London. She made the move to Buckinghamshire and went on to have a girl, followed by a boy, and settled into life as a full-time mum. When her son was about a year old, Kate knew it was time for her to work again in some capacity. In her own words, she'd found being a full-time mum 'the hardest job' she'd ever done. For Kate, photography became the stop gap between being there for her children full-time and going back to work. It started as a hobby and soon became an obsession, with those closest to her suggesting she made this her new career instead of returning to the corporate world.

Kate found it became the new focus for her life. Having always worked in creative industries in managerial roles, she was now able to do the creating herself. For her, people photography is extremely rewarding because clients are delighted to be given images that stop time and explore human relationships.

Coming from a family of high achievers, Kate's Why became the desire to succeed so she didn't have to return to the daily grind of corporate life.

Working for herself also meant that those who would gain from the long hours and hard work would be her family, rather than a board of directors.

So, she improved her photography skills and knowledge through training and education and, with her background, invested in developing a professional brand so her business was positioned in the market exactly where she wanted to be. She went on to successfully leverage PR using styled shoots to highlight her expertise. It wasn't long before she'd secured herself a monthly column in an influential industry magazine, was hosting packed seminars at photography events, and had moved into mentoring fellow photographers to enhance their skills.

Kate will be the first to admit that those initial days and months of launching her business were hard. As she had a young family and was working around their needs, it often meant late nights and snatched moments, but she found it was amazing to see what could be achieved with limited time when she became focused.

It wasn't long before she became an Ambassador for Nikon (a position held by only a handful of professional photographers), and now, having made the switch to Sony, she and her husband Brent are Sony European Imaging Ambassadors, providing a mix of photography, film, and training between them.

The one thing that Kate says you need more than anything else is a support network. She still finds getting the balance between being there for everyone and dedicating the amount of time to her business can be tricky, but she wouldn't change a thing. She knows that she's passing on the work ethic to her children and teaching them to be independent and ambitious. And perhaps just as importantly, her daily commute is just walking to the studio at the bottom of her garden, from where she works.

When Kate first began her journey, her Why stemmed from the basic needs to feed, clothe, and house her children. She wanted to maintain financial independence and it became her reason for keeping on going. Although the mum guilt is ever present, she will be the first to say you shouldn't beat yourself up about it. Running any business is an enormous undertaking and takes constant work but she's managing to do so on her own terms and to make it work for her and her family.

Hopefully, Kate's example has inspired you as you now sit and focus on your own Why. Kate has been a huge inspiration to me and is my go-to for family photographs. One of the ones she took of my family when J was just four months old, sits proudly framed on our lounge wall at home. She's truly in a class of her own.

Kate Kirkman - Owner of Kate Hopewell-Smith Photography and Training by Lumiere LTD

(www.katehopewellsmith.com)

* * *

2

THE PR STORYTELLING
FRAMEWORK™

WHAT IT IS AND HOW IT CAN HELP YOU

B efore we get into the important elements that you need to have in place for securing PR, I want to introduce you to The PR Storytelling Framework™, which I've devised to help you with this whole process.

As you will have already gathered, I'm a firm believer that story-telling should be at the heart of not only any PR you secure, but also any communications you have with your audience. This should include any emails that you send, social media posts you create, and any other marketing that you use to connect more fully with them.

It is through stories that you can effectively engage with them. The more people know about your brand or product, the more likely they are to make the decision to buy what you have to sell. In this way, the number of people you're able to help and there-fore impact, will increase. And through this, you will also be able to effectively grow and scale your business.

S – Storytelling not Selling

We will cover this in a later chapter but please don't approach everything from the point of view of a sale. No one wants to feel like they're constantly being sold to. As an entrepreneur, the importance of maximising the online space has never been more important. Those who already had an online offering at the start of the pandemic, saw their businesses growing. There is no escaping the fact you now have to have an online presence and with your website as your shop window, make sure you reflect who you are and what you do in as appealing a way as possible

T – Talk to your audience about YOU!

Please don't shy away from your brand reflecting your personality. Think Sir Richard Branson and Virgin or the late Steve Jobs and Apple. Share your journey and why you do what you do, not just hiding behind marketing messages.

O – Opportunities

Sometimes a media interview will come along, and it can feel like it's hard work. You might have to juggle some client calls around, find a last-minute babysitter, or travel to be somewhere just to make it happen. Is it worth it? Nine times out of ten, yes. Why? You never know who else will see that interview or hear you speak on that radio station. I've lost count of the number of additional opportunities that clients have secured as a direct result of being more visible through the power of PR, including book deals and speaking gigs.

R – Research your media

I talk about this in more depth throughout this book, but there's no quick fix to knowing the media. You can't expect someone to have you onto their podcast as a guest if you haven't bothered to listen to at least two episodes and have thought through what value you can offer their audience. It's the same when approaching a journalist. Make sure you're aware of the publication they write for, or any pieces they have recently been working on. It can really help in terms of them being more open to responding to any initial email that you send.

Y – You!

In the same way that you should talk to your audience about yourself and the journey you have been on, don't be afraid to tell them a bit about you. It doesn't mean you have to share everything. Think about your values and those of your business. Is honesty and authenticity important to you? Then show them that through how you communicate with them and harness the power of PR to work in the same way.

T – Trust yourself, you can do this!

I get how scary it can feel at first to step out of your comfort zone and start securing PR. But as a founder of your own business, you have already come much further than so many others. Now you're just harnessing PR to be able to help you reach and impact others, to help them through what you do. You have so got this and if you're still feeling stuck refer to any of the sections in this book to help you take another step forward.

E – Expertise

You really are an expert in your field. Now you just need to show up, own your expert status by securing media trust tags so you can display the logos of the publications on your website to highlight your credibility. All those hours you put into training to become the best at what you do? Those qualifications that you have secured? That website that speaks volumes about the time and skills needed to get to where you are? Those are all markers for your expertise. Now you just need to cement it all, through PR.

L – Let people know how you can help them

If no one knows what you do why would they come looking for you? Don't expect people to be falling over themselves to work with you the minute your flash new website goes live. You have to tell them how they can work with you and make it as simple as possible to be found. That way when they have a problem, they know you're the right fit for them. But if you don't tell them, they will just look elsewhere.

L – Learn what makes great content for journalists

Again, this comes down to research. Make sure you don't just fire off an email pitching yourself before you have looked at or familiarised yourself with the content in the publication. Think about the stories you enjoy reading, watching, or listening to. Then think about why it's of interest and how what you have to share could fit in or be something different or equally valuable.

I – Ideal clients and where they hang out

Knowing who you're trying to reach with your communications is key in terms of successful PR. There's no point just adopting a spray and pray method of trying to secure coverage. Gone are the days when you could just write a press release and hope a journalist would pick up on what you have to say. Please don't underestimate the importance of knowing your ideal clients. I've even created a FREE workbook to help you if you haven't already identified who you want to be aiming your business communications at. You can download it here:

www.njrpr.com/book

N – Never give up!

PR is like a trail of breadcrumbs. It takes time for you to see true tangible results from all your efforts, so it's important to never give up. It can be tempting to throw the towel when you don't hear back from a journalist after two weeks of sending them an email. But journalists are just like you and me. They're extremely busy juggling lots of competing deadlines and they might not have seen the last message you sent them. The key is always to never give up. I've lost count of the number of times that emails have gone unanswered or when I first started in PR, the number of times a phone call to a national news desk was abruptly ended. If I can do it, so can you!

G – Go for opportunities

Going for PR opportunities is important especially when you're initially nervous about even getting visible in the first place. But please make sure that anything you put yourself forward for, is aligned to you, your brand, and your values. Think about where you want to be seen and then take the steps to get there. This book will also help you with each of the stages of your journey.

Now it's down to you to effectively grow and scale your business through strategic PR storytelling. Don't forget there are many ways in which you can do this, it's not just through the media – though I have to say, combined with writing a book and speaking on stages, it's one of my favourite ways to get visible and get known for what you do.

3

WHAT NEEDS TO BE IN PLACE

Now that you have decided you want to secure some PR to raise awareness about your business and what you do, it can feel tempting to just rush straight into contacting a couple of journalists, especially if you see suitable requests. But before you do this, please ensure that you have a few things in place.

What would happen if you sent an email and a journalist (who is likely to be working to a tight deadline) responds, and asks you for some comments, professional images, and a short biography all to be sent back within the hour. Trust me, this happens, especially when writers are working for national publications.

Will you be able to ensure that you get to say everything that you want to? Will you have capacity to rummage around and find where you put those all-important professional images in high resolution and send back your biography along with your comments highlighting your expertise within that timeframe?

Don't put so much pressure on yourself. Instead, have a folder on your computer desktop containing the following:

- Your story (already written)
- Professional images (in both landscape and portrait)
- A long and short version of your biography (already written)
- Notes about what messaging is important so you never leave anything out in any interview

Let's look at each of the above in more detail to help you gather everything together ahead of time.

YOUR STORY

There's nothing more important than both knowing and having your story written down and presented in such a way that a journalist can clearly see the angles contained within it. This really can make the difference between you being over-looked for an opportunity or being accepted. Lots of PRs skip this step and think that instead, a lengthy media bio will suffice. What you need to know is that a journalist is looking for easy to disseminate information. Don't make them wade through more than a page of text to work out what your story is. Have it already written. The success rate of my clients speaks volumes as to why this approach works. An important thing to mention here is that your story is just that. No one else can own it or have it, as you and you alone have had the experiences that make your journey unique. It's by far your greatest asset and your biggest selling point. So why would you want to overlook it, or have it hastily cobbled together instead of taking the time to map it out and understand exactly what it is and how it can help you help others?

Before I go any further let me explain the two types of earned PR. There is reactive PR – where a journalist is actively looking for a case study or an expert and they post a request on a database or Twitter saying what they're looking for. Then, there is pro-active PR, which involves you putting yourself forward to a journalist/editor asking them to run a part of your story. It could be your whole story or an element of it, and pro-active pitching takes the longest time, and can be much harder to secure pieces from. The reason being, you're asking the publication to consider running your story when they might not have been planning anything along those lines. You also have to think about what's known as lead times.

As a rough guide they are as follows:

- Glossy monthly magazines – some work six months ahead (Christmas in July – it really is a thing, especially for titles like BBC's *Good Food* magazine). *Psychologies* is up to four months in advance and *Red*, *Prima* and *Good Housekeeping* work three months ahead.
- *Grazia* – two weeks in advance and the print version is fortnightly too. The online site is more fluid in terms of case studies and what it's looking to cover.
- *Stylist* – the team works four weeks in advance for all versions, even digital and the podcast.
- Women's weekly magazines – work a month ahead (and even more at Christmas).
- National newspapers – features can be a few days beforehand / national news stories the day before.
- Online sites – can be instantaneous but sometimes also need a bit of planning. Don't rely on something being turned around straight away as journalists are inherently busy.
- TV – will film on the day for that day's news but booking

guests for shows like ITV's *This Morning* or *The One Show* on BBC One can be anything up to three or four weeks in advance.

- Radio – booking guests in advance, sometimes two to three days or more beforehand, but if they have an interview slot you can be in luck for an opportunity on the day, although this is becoming rarer.
- Bloggers – like to have all information at least a week in advance, if not more.
- Podcasts – you can apply and successfully record a podcast interview, but it might not air until a few months down the line because of the schedule. It's worth asking when it will be released so you can prepare your audience in advance.

So, now you understand the different types of earned PR that we're going to explore in this chapter, hopefully you're starting to understand why it's important to know your story inside out. Once it's written, it will allow you to respond to any media requests or to pitch yourself out quickly and in a timeframe that could work for the publication you're approaching. But always remember to think about why the media should care about your story. What is it that will make it work for them, and why should they run it at any particular moment in time?

SEARCH ENGINE OPTIMISATION (SEO)

Search Engine Optimisation or SEO is also important to consider when it comes to securing any media coverage because it is very much part of the PR planning process. As much as you want to be telling your story, you need to do so in a way that balances being engaging and making sure that you and your business are easily found online. This will include making sure that the sites or publications you choose to focus on securing coverage with have a great DA (Domain Authority) score. Why is this important? As a business owner, you want to be found so you can attract more clients and reach more of the people that need what you have to offer. Websites that have higher scores tend to have a higher ranking in search engines such as Google and Yahoo. As a guide, a DA between forty and fifty is considered average, between fifty and sixty is good and anything sixty-plus is great. In short, the higher the DA score, the more likely those sites are to receive more or better web traffic. The majority of national newspaper and magazine online sites will have DA scores above seventy.

PROFESSIONAL IMAGES

 "There can be no words without pictures."

— *ARISTOTLE.*

I can't stress enough the importance of having professional images that showcase both yourself and what you do. If, on receiving a pitch from you, a journalist looks at your website and sees that you have a series of badly taken images on a mobile phone, or your brand doesn't look professional enough, what do you think they will do? Look elsewhere! We all know that first impressions count, and with your images being part and parcel of that first impression, there is nothing more important than getting this right. Journalists are busy. They get around five hundred emails a day, and if they're actively looking for a case study, who do you think they will select? Someone who has submitted a couple of selfies, or someone who has invested in a professional photographer who understands depth of field, great camera angles and the importance of light?

It's rare that a newspaper will want to run images taken at night too. Why? Because of the prohibitive printing cost for additional black ink. So, concentrate instead on having a collection of images that are both landscape and portrait, reflect you both working in/on your business (i.e., if you're a florist, it's a no-brainer to have images of you picking/holding up flowers), some other lifestyle images, a couple of alternative headshots and any other images that sum up your story over the years. These images are known as collects and will help take someone through each stage of your journey. For example, if your story begins when you're small, you should have an image of you as a child. If your story involves someone else and they're still alive, please check that you have their permission to mention them, and that any photos of them are also okay to be used. Sometimes Picture Editors will happily pixilate out the person's face, but you have to ensure you're covered in all circumstances, legally speaking, which means there's no redress on you or the publication should that person in question complain.

That's why when it comes to more sensitive stories, such as domestic abuse or sexual assaults, sometimes it's worth not mentioning the person's relationship to you, and instead just alluding to what happened or being generic with any mention of how you knew them. For instance, if you have just left your husband, you could just speak of an abusive relationship as that could have happened at any point in your past.

In terms of the quality and size of images, they should all be around 1mb/2mb in size and 300 dpi, which is the required quality for any print titles. Images for online sites can be slightly less, but good quality images that highlight your story throughout will always be preferred.

When it comes to some dos and don'ts for choosing a professional photographer here are some guidelines for you:

DO:

- Check out their previous work so you understand their style and how the images will look.
- Plan any brand shoot in advance, knowing the location and look and feel.
- Have a consultation with your photographer beforehand so you're fully happy.
- Plan your outfits for what you want from the pictures.
- Have a change of outfit so that you get different looks and feels to your images.
- Have your hair / make-up done and any blemishes covered.
- Re-schedule if heavy downpours are expected and you're planning an outdoor shoot.

DON'T:

- Just rock up on the day and expect your photographer to understand what it is you're after.
- Try to wing it in terms of location only to find there are roadworks on site.
- Wear intricate patterns or stripes.
- Just guess the kind of image you're looking to portray to your audience.
- Wear something that you later regret and then can't use the images as a result.
- Have anything nearby with logos or cartoon characters

on. It could cause problems in terms of PR because it could be an infringement on another brand's Intellectual Property, known as IP.

It's worth also considering hiring a place on Air B n B or similar for the day if you want a specific look or feel to your images. Investing in professional hair and make-up can also make an enormous difference to how your images reflect you as the face of your business.

Here are some thoughts from professional photographer Amanda Hutchinson, who runs AKP Branding Stories:

The biggest mistakes I see...

First, don't try to be something you're not in your photos. I can see how it happens. You see all these images on Pinterest and social media of a certain type of image and think that you also have to do that pose. If you don't drink coffee, you don't need to be sitting drinking coffee in your brand photos!

There's a mistake I see before people even come to me, and that's the belief that a phone photo or selfie is sufficient for their brand imagery. In the online world we live in, our audience and potential clients expect us to take our business as seriously as we want them to, and that means showing images that are high quality, as well as being representative of who we really are. And a poor-quality selfie just doesn't cut the mustard anymore, and certainly won't have the press banging on your door to feature you.

I would always advise...

Before you even engage with a brand photographer, make sure you really understand your brand messages and the story you want portrayed. This step alone will make sure that your photos are synonymous with your brand and who you are. It's those images that captivate your audience and draw them in.

Then, when it comes to choosing a photographer, I always advise that you have a call with any you have shortlisted (and choose them based on their style and approach so it aligns with your brand aesthetic). It's important to work with someone who not only understands your brand story and vision, but that you feel comfortable and at ease with. You need to be able to trust your photographer as any unease or tension you feel will show in your face on the day of the shoot. Your eyes just won't have that sparkle, even if you're smiling.

Other thoughts...

Your brand images are an investment in your business, so make sure they're working hard for you. Talk to your brand photographer about the plans you have for PR, marketing, launches and anything else exciting you have coming up in your business, as this will mean they're able to help you have a treasure chest of photos that will help you grow your business.

Amanda Hutchinson - AKP Branding Stories

(www.akpbrandingstories.co.uk)

YOUR BIOGRAPHY

It's always recommended that you have both a short and a longer version of your biography written in advance before you even start reaching out to anyone for PR. The reason being, if a journalist comes to you and says, "Can you please send me a short bio of you so that we can include it as part of your piece that you have written?" you're not scrambling around trying to write everything right at the last minute. The best way to write a short bio is always to write it in the third person. Using me as an example, it would read along the following lines:

Nicola J Rowley has worked in the media for over twenty-five years, both as a journalist and award-winning PR manager. She now runs her own communications agency called NJRPR and specialises in helping female entrepreneurs and brands in the leisure and entertainment industry get visible through strategic PR storytelling.

Something like the above is all you need for a short biography – two to three sentences linked together and straight to the point. The longer version of your biography can then go into your achievements, awards that you have won, the places you have worked. If, like me, you have worked internationally, you could say something like...

Nicola J Rowley has worked in the media for over twenty-five years, both nationally and internationally both as a journalist and mutli-award-winning PR expert.

The most important thing is to know that you have said everything that you want to, and nothing has been missed out. Have an up-to-date copy of your CV next to you when you write it, or you could make a list of your achievements and tick them off as you include them. Another good tip to writing a great biography is to go onto the website of a well-known person or personality that you admire, or find their agent who represents them, and have a look at their biography. This way, you won't be sharing everything, but just the important parts that should be highlighted and will make it more compelling for a journalist to speak to or feature you.

Perhaps in your spare time, you have raised thousands of pounds for a specific charity, and you are well known for that within your field, as well as outside of it. Obviously if you have only raised a few hundred pounds because you ran a marathon once, I'm not sure that should make the final edit, but you get the gist. You want to be putting in all your achievements and tying it together, so that when people read it, they're like, okay now I feel like I know more about this person. What I will say about your biography, is that it **isn't** your story. Your story is very different to your biography.

When I'm writing a client's story for them, following a Strategy Session, I would never mention that someone has won a specific award unless there's a reason for it. I might say they're a multi-award-winning independent financial advisor, or I might say they're a well-known psychologist, but I wouldn't explain it in the same way as a biography. A biography is far more factual and straight to the point.

Your story is much more of a piecing together of the jigsaw puzzle, so that every part of your journey slots into place and fits.

When writing your biography, keep your sentences short and don't overcomplicate anything more than it needs to be. It's always worth reading anything you write aloud so you can hear any mistakes or anything that doesn't sound right and correct things as you go along.

It's also important to keep the language you use as simple as possible. Your biography needs to read as if you were talking to a friend in the pub. For example, if you're a hair stylist specialising in weddings – don't call yourself a refiner of tresses. If you run a dog grooming business – you are not a pamperer of poodles (I mean, you probably are but I think you understand where I'm coming from). It's important that it resonates with everyone.

If you have impacted the lives of ten thousand children through what it is that you do, or helped hundreds of people with stress and anxiety, that is worth a mention in your biography. The most important thing is that you want to be able to present a professional, and yet amazing biography, that really shows how much you shine within your chosen field.

IDEAL CLIENTS

As a small business owner, there is nothing more important for you to understand than your ideal clients. These are the people that are going to want to work with you. They're the people who are actively looking for you. And they're also going to be the ones that will resonate the most with you and your story. Take time to really build up a picture of who they are, where they spend time together, what do they do, and know their likes and dislikes.

Knowing what media they consume is important. What newspapers do they read online or in print? What magazines do they like to thumb through on a regular basis? Which podcasts do they download and what TV and radio do they watch and listen to?

Once you have this greater understanding of where they're spending time together or what they're reading and doing, it will give you more of an idea about which publications you should be aiming to be featured in or on, because this is how you can highlight what it is you do and then go on to help them the most.

This is why knowing your ideal clients is such an important foundation for your business. Not just in terms of securing PR, but in general. Ideally, you need to create a picture of them that you understand inside out. When it comes to sharing your message about what you do, knowing all this information will enable you to reach them more easily and go on to impact their lives.

It's also worth thinking about their pain points. What is causing them confusion, concern, or stress right now? How can you help them solve that issue? It's worth also knowing how you can prove this is the case. If your ideal clients are busy and don't have much time, where do they get their news? If you're not sure, if you already have a group of clients just ask them. That way, you will know where you should be aiming to be seen/heard and where your ideal client is likely to find you. Building up a picture of your ideal client in this way is known as an avatar. It allows you to identify with them more readily and will allow you to become more focused in how you reach them and hopefully go on to help them solve their problems.

An example for a working mum ideal client avatar would be:

This is Kate. She's in her thirties and is a working mum who has returned to work recently after having either one or two children. She is struggling/feeling lost. She feels torn because she's missing seeing her children grow up. She is still career focused, in that she needs an outlet away from her family (she used to be ambitious in a corporate sense, now she's ambitious for her family). She has a lot of friends, but she is feeling isolated. She lives just outside of a major city and commutes into work. She's a strong character and knows her own mind. She wants to maintain her independence but not at the cost of her children. Her confidence levels are not where they should be. She loves to travel and have lovely holidays. Job wise, she is in a well-paid job, maybe at a university or in Marketing, and has done well to get to where she has. But she's surrounded by people who don't get that she's a mum too. She knows there's more out there and wants to find out what her options are and how she can make a change in her life as soon as possible.

If you need some more guidance around your ideal clients, I've created a FREE Ideal Client workbook which will take you through the exercises you can use to identify their needs, wants and desires. **You can download it by visiting:**

www.njrpr.com/book

Now you hopefully have an idea of the kind of titles they like to read, listen to or watch, please do your research. Have a look at the magazines, the newspapers, the supplements that come with the newspapers. Do they have any regular features that could work for you and where your business could be mentioned, or you could provide an expert comment? Sometimes with small business owners, we're guilty of thinking that our ideal clients are only interested in reading about the industry that we work in. But everyone has hobbies and interests outside of what they do, and everyone has a guilty pleasure or finds out about the news in a certain way. Nine times out of ten, they will be looking at traditional media rather than just reading industry specific titles.

As part of your work in identifying your ideal client, you also need to work out where they spend time together. An effective way to look at this is to think about where they do their weekly food shop. For instance, as a rule of thumb, if they shop at Waitrose, they're likely to be reading the *Daily Mail*, *The Daily Telegraph* or *The Guardian*. Do they shop at Tesco? If so, then they're more likely to read *The Sun, Daily Mirror,* and other more populist titles with mass appeal. Have a think about where you want to position yourself and your business.

Do you want to be reaching more people on a wider scale, for instance, with *The Sun?* They are firm supporters of female entrepreneurs. They also have a big focus on reaching mums so a lot of their content, especially online, will be focused on things like celebrating female entrepreneurs through features such as *'Bossing It with Karren Brady',* and highlighting how brilliant a certain business is when someone reaches that six-figure mark. Don't discount pieces like this as, through doing them, you can resonate with your audience on a much wider scale.

When it comes to *Mail Online,* it is now the world's biggest website. So yes, you do want to be seen on *Mail Online,* whether or not you think you do. It's a guilty pleasure that not everyone admits to scrolling through, but it's too important to ignore its reach or the potential impact it could have on your business. And yes, it also has one of the biggest DA scores too, so it works particularly well for that all-important SEO.

When it comes to getting to know your ideal client, please make sure you put them at the heart of everything that you do. Getting visible is no longer about you, it's about how you can help them. Find out more about them, understand them. It's no good doing a spray and pray marketing offensive, where you just go out there and say yes, I appeal to everyone. Having a niche is a good thing. Any PR that you secure should be strategically focused on the people that will buy from you, the people that you can help, and the impact that you can have on their lives. That is who you should be trying to reach through what it is you do. And that's when the power of PR comes into its own. Surely, being able to help and impact the life of just one person makes this whole entrepreneurial roller coaster worthwhile?

Don't forget you can download your FREE Ideal Client workbook by visiting:

www.njrpr.com/book

4

GETTING STRATEGIC

When it comes to your PR strategy, it should go hand in hand with your business strategy and compliment your content plan. Above all, think about the following:

- What do you want to talk about (this is your story)?
- What are you going to do throughout the year?
- What do you want to highlight and for when?
- What do you want any PR to achieve? Is it a mix of awareness, new members, new clients?

KEY MESSAGES

Sitting alongside your story are your key messages. These can be woven into any interviews that you secure to ensure you always get the outcome that you're after. After all, there's no point completing an interview and realising that it didn't pay back to your business or help let those all-important ideal clients know how you can help them.

So, what is your messaging?

I'd always advise that you have three messages prepared in advance of speaking to any journalist. Some examples are below, which you can adapt for yourself and your business:

- **I specialise in helping female entrepreneurs get visible using strategic PR storytelling.**
- **Sharing your story enables you to connect at a much deeper level with your audience and the work I do helps women unlock their stories, so they secure more media exposure – and in turn, help others.**
- **You can find out more about me at my website: www.njrpr.com.**

For any interview, have your key messages printed out or on post it notes where you can see them. It's too easy to get carried away when you speak to journalists and then realise afterwards that you didn't say what you wanted to, or worse still, you over-shared information you didn't mean to. This is why having your key messages already sorted beforehand can, in many cases, become a PR lifesaver.

Conversely, if you tend to over-share things, make a list of what you shouldn't talk about and have that somewhere you can see it when you speak to any journalist too.

BUSINESS OBJECTIVES

When it comes to being strategic, the next step is to think about your business goals and take your lead from there. If you're not sure about what they should be, a good way to start is to think about how much money you would like to make in the next twelve months, six months and so on, and then look at what you want your business model to look like.

By this, I mean there's no point being a wedding photographer or planner if you cherish spending time with your school-age children, as you will have to sacrifice a lot of your weekends. Perhaps now you're running your own business, you want to only work the equivalent of school hours and not at all during the holidays. Or perhaps you want to only work four days a week and have Friday off to spend as you would like to. Whatever works best for you, fit your business objectives around that, and please don't make the common mistake of working so hard to get everything off the ground that you burn out.

Business goals should also be SMART – which means: Specific, Measurable, Achievable, Realistic, and work within a set Timeframe. There's no point saying you want to achieve something but then not have a way to measure if you have been successful, or a set time within which you will reach it.

Some suggested business goals could include:

- In January 2022, my book about *The Power of PR* will be published and as a result, I will see a 50% uplift in sales and enquiries compared to the same time last year
- At the end of January 2022, I will launch my signature course – *PR Mastery, The Course* and will double the number of people who join the VIP tier compared to the last time that I launched

When it comes to your business objectives, you need to already be thinking about the next six months ahead and the more established you are, start planning even further down the line, such as a year. I must admit, I like to have a plan for an entire year and then work out exactly when I'm going to launch a course or an offering. There is, of course, nothing to say this plan has to stay exactly as it is. It just means you have a framework to work from. But of course, it's your plan, so you can change things when any unforeseen circumstances come along (pandemic, anyone?).

Sit down and look at key dates. Anything that is highlighted on your calendar that you want to be present for, such as birthdays and anniversaries. Think about the school holidays if you have children, or breaks away, or key moments that you will need to avoid. Then work backwards from there in terms of developing your business strategy. This way your business is starting to take shape around your life, and not the other way around.

Going back to the monetary objective, work out how much you would like to make in the next six months. How much would you like to be turning over in the next year? Then have a look at what you're currently offering right now in terms of your services or products and work out how many of those will you need to sell to be able to reach your end goal. If the figures don't add up, or the numbers of clients you will need are unrealistic, think about raising your prices to make it all fit together or introduce a new offer that will help you out.

Now you need to start thinking about how you're going to reach your audience and let them know that you have this offer so you're able to then reach them more effectively.

Then, you need to work backwards again and start thinking about the content that you're going to be creating. This includes talking around the themes of the product or the service or the course or membership and this should be the common theme in all your content.

For example, when I'm looking to re-open the doors to my online *PR Mastery Membership*, a few weeks beforehand I start talking about the successes that current members have had, and the difference it's made to both them and, in turn, their clients.

Nearer to launch, I'll talk about the importance of building relationships with journalists (highlighting that we have monthly Q&A sessions in the membership with national journalists).

And then, when the doors open to the membership, I speak to members who have been on a journey with me through PR. We find out how having real-time media requests, with journalist contact details provided directly to them, alongside strategic PR advice and handholding, has made a huge difference to them.

It's simple. Base your content around your plan. And base your PR around your plan too – so that everything strategically aligns to work in your favour.

When it comes to launching a new service or product, this is when you need to be thinking about visibility, because the more eyes that you have on you at that time, the more people will hear about you and what you do. This can all be done organically if you maximise the power of PR.

COMMUNICATIONS OBJECTIVES

Like anything in your business, having objectives is necessary and this goes for your communications too. These should highlight the key moments when you will also be doing other activities; so, say you're planning to sell a course in Q1, say in January, then in Q2, April, and again around Q4, October, you should be looking to set objectives for how many pieces of PR you would like to secure for each of these times, as well as what your target publications are.

Begin by thinking about the topics that you already know you're an expert on.

- Which publications would you like to be seen in or on?
- Are national newspapers and magazines more of a priority than online sites?
- Is your aim to be seen on television?
- Do you want to be featured on at least twelve podcasts, for instance?
- Do you want to be featured in at least two magazines?

Then, just as before, work backwards and come up with a plan to be able to make that happen, for those podcasts and for those publications to come out around the time of your launch. Think about how your Communications Objectives can help you support your Business Objectives, and as before, they need to be SMART.

For instance, when looking at your Business Objectives, now consider the following:

What: Think about the outcome / impact you want to have with any PR.

Who: This will be your target audience.

How much: How will you measure your success (this is known as metrics, and some are listed below)?

When: Decide on a specific timeframe by when you would like the objective to be achieved.

A good example could be:

- Reach XX% target audience with at least XX pieces of coverage containing key messages over the next six months

If you're also focusing on social media activity at the same time:

- XX% increase in positive engagement on related social posts over the next six months.

Measuring success

I mentioned metrics and by these, I mean the following:

- The number of PR items generated
- Social posts and tweets that enhance your activity
- E-mail marketing numbers (audience building and open rates of your emails)
- Click-throughs to your website
- Number of people attending events
- The number of messages placed through PR coverage
- How many opportunities have been generated through PR activity

Refer to Chapter Three of this book where I've talked about publication times. As a rule of thumb, for the women's glossy magazines such as *Red*, *Good Housekeeping* and *Psychologies*, you're looking at between three to four months ahead, *Stylist* is four weeks, national newspapers can be the day before, but features can be a few days and up to a couple of weeks, and online can be much more flexible and immediate. When it comes to podcasts, they may record them around the time you're looking for them to go live, but bear in mind, they may not go out for another few months. So, if you're planning to do a big burst of podcast interviews, you need to ensure you know when your episode is going out and agree that in advance with the host. There's no point doing an interview, it sporadically appears, but doesn't tie in with anything else that you're doing, and it doesn't pay back to having that visibility around the time when you are launching. Of course, as with everything, there are always caveats to this. If a publication is huge i.e., *Forbes* or *BBC Radio Five Live*, do the interview anyway, as it will enhance your reputation and increase your reach. And it means you can have those all-important media trust tags (logos from the media outlets) displayed prominently on your website.

Having goals in place and setting your intentions is hugely important when it comes to business and for securing PR. It's like anything, if you have a focus and you have set time-specific goals, you know when you want to be able to achieve something and it gives you something to aim for.

For example, if you just say, I have a goal to run a half marathon, as it's open ended, you may well lose focus when it comes to training. But instead, if you say, I want to be able to run a half marathon by the end of April and we're in January, then you can effectively map out the steps you need to take to reach that point.

For instance, look at how fit you currently are and think how much running you need to do to feel confident that you can finish a half marathon by the end of April, and not injure yourself in the process. Your plan begins with running for thirty minutes a day and building up from there. By the start of March, you will be running for an hour and a half. Then, you will find that you're much closer to reaching your goal.

Just as an aside (and not business related at all), once you can quite comfortably run six miles, you will be able to run a half marathon. I know this because I once interviewed and went running with Steve Cram and I was worried about my training. And knowing that he's the expert in his field, I listened to what he said. And yes, I ran my first half marathon testing this as a theory and yes, it works. I had previously only ever run six miles, but on the day, I was fine.

Once you have drawn up a plan and a strategic target list, it's important that you stick to it, where possible.

Whilst running your own business, there are so many competing demands on your time, and it's easy to allow any of your media outreach to be the first thing that slides. But not prioritising PR is a big mistake.

- How else are your ideal clients going to get to know about you?
- How else are your ideal clients going to realise you're the expert they need to work with?
- How else are your ideal clients going to see that you're the person who's going to solve the problem they currently have?

And remember, you owe it to that person that really needs you to stick to your goals, to focus on your plan and to follow through. If you carve out just an hour a week for making proactive PR approaches, you are much more likely to get success, because an hour a week is four hours a month. You can do three pitches a week, which multiplied by four is twelve. That's twelve separate pitches put forward to different media outlets that will be read or seen or listened to by your ideal clients. So, you can see, it's perfectly possible to do this.

Set aside the time. Plan. See it through and make it happen.

The starting point for everything is to be clear on your story. Then, be clear on when you want the coverage to appear. Know what you want the outcome of any piece to be (through using your key messages).

For instance, say you're bringing out a course around beating imposter syndrome. You want to be talking about the time when you really struggled with imposter syndrome and that moment when you had the realisation you could no longer stand in your own way. This is the kind of thing you need to be talking about, to enable you to resonate with your ideal clients, and the clients that are then going to look at your website and see that you have a course, all about imposter syndrome. Remember that trail of PR breadcrumbs.

This means that you need to ensure that ahead of any launch, your website (which is in effect your shop front) is as up to date as possible and is pointing to the one thing you want people to see when they visit it.

Business case study

Lisa Johnson - Business Strategist

Lisa Johnson's story is nothing short of inspirational. She began her first business as a wedding planner, £30k in debt, and within four years has gone on to become a multi-millionaire, working as a Business Strategist, helping other entrepreneurs launch courses and memberships. During the pandemic, Lisa bucked the trend and went on to have three of the biggest online course launches in the UK in quick succession.

That's a very short summary of Lisa's story but you can already see how that would make a compelling read and it's why Lisa has been featured in *Forbes, Metro, The Daily Telegraph, Mail Online, The Sun Online, Express.co.uk, Refinery29, Female First, We Are The City* (as an inspirational woman) and interviewed on BBC Radio Five Live and TALK Radio (those pieces, with the exception of *Forbes*, are just the ones I've arranged for her). She has been in many more publications, and on several influential podcasts besides, because she understands the power of PR in growing her business and her brand. In deciding to get visible strategically, Lisa has successfully scaled her business to what it is today.

And because she understands the importance of PR, if you send her an opportunity to write something for an interview to be completed at short notice, she finds the time in her schedule to prioritise it. We'll come on to it later when we talk about what journalists want, but in short, they want someone like Lisa. She has a great understanding of her story and the angles that could work for the media. She's reliable and professional. And she will happily meet any deadline, even if that does mean speaking to the late show on *BBC Radio Five Live* about online bullying and how her *Forbes* article went viral at midnight or doing an interview at short notice whilst driving across a glacier in Iceland! She gets that media exposure not only raises her credibility, but like her full-page feature in *Metro,* her recent page lead piece in *The Daily Telegraph* or her anti-bullying opinion piece in *Metro*, it translates into more followers and more potential clients.

The thing that Lisa is well known for (aside from passive income and launching) is strategy. She strategically plans her year in advance, and so knows when she will be looking for more awareness around what she's planning to do. It means that all her marketing, including any PR approaches or efforts, can be made ahead of time. There is no way around it – being strategic about your PR to help you reach your business goals is key to success.

What has leveraging the power of PR meant for you?

It's meant that people have been able to get to know me more deeply. With PR, someone that has no knowledge of me can hear a part of my story and relate to it in some way. We all know that there are millions of people doing what each of us does. What will make a person work with you over someone else is you as a person and your story. So, you need to get it out there!

Why is PR so important in raising your profile as a business owner?

It gives you credibility. It's as simple as that. And different people see credibility in different places. For instance, when I'm in *Metro*, then my old corporate colleagues think I've made it, but it took me being in *The Daily Telegraph* and *The Guardian* for my dad to think I actually have a business rather than play on the internet all day! And for others, my *Forbes* article and *Business Insider* pieces meant they respected my views more because both of those publications make you prove your earnings, so it was a nod to people realising I wasn't just making my figures up.

It's important to be in a cross section of titles to raise your profile.

How do you think PR has made a difference to you and your business?

It's done a few things: it's helped others take my business and knowledge seriously. It's meant more clients have found me, but it's also attracted new opportunities that I didn't know would happen. I was in an article that someone read. They then realised, a few months later, my podcast had made it to number one in the UK business charts. They listened to it, got to know me, and then offered me a lucrative book deal. I also received another offer from one of the biggest publishing houses in the world, the week afterwards. You never know where things will take you when it comes to PR.

What would be your advice to anyone just starting out in their business journey when it comes to PR?

Don't wait until you feel like the 'guru' or expert. You will never feel like that! Show others what you know and how you can help and let them decide if you're the expert.

Lisa Johnson - Business Strategist (www.lisajohnson.com)

* * *

Now that you have successfully planned out your goals, you need to make a start to make them a reality. Remember, it's ok to not have all the answers at this stage. Rarely do we know how anything is going to pan out. But by taking that initial leap of faith and stepping into action taking mode, you're at least ensuring that you're heading in the right direction. The key to everything is getting started.

Let me ask you this: has there been something that you have been meaning to do, that you have never yet quite got around to? If so, what have you used as the excuse? Has it been because you were afraid of what others might say? Scared that you might fail? Fearful of what the results might be? Or simply, have you thought, "Oh yes, I must do that," and then been sidetracked by the busyness of life or by the needs of your partner or family?

There is no kind way to put this: anything that you haven't started and then gone on to finish - that book you've been meaning to write, that job you wished you had applied for - they're now all missed opportunities. And these opportunities didn't happen because you were standing in your own way.

What do I mean by this? Well, at the time when you made the decision not to do that one thing you thought you should do, you were in effect looking at things almost back to front. I'm sure that on some level, you came up with excuses as to why these things couldn't happen and reasoned with yourself that you were fine with where you were and didn't have enough time anyway, instead of putting on your big girl pants and getting things done.

Let me ask you this, when you think about that book you still haven't written, that job you wished you'd applied for, that opportunity that passed you by – how do you feel? Do you regret any of it? Do you now wish you had given it a go to see where it may have taken you?

The harsh reality is this: life isn't a dress rehearsal where we can come back and have more time to get things done. We have one life, and that life is short.

Excuses are just that, excuses. At least if you have put one foot in front of the other and given something a go, that's something. At least you can say, "I tried, but on this occasion, it didn't quite work out the way I wanted it to. But that's ok because I tried."

So, when you find yourself on the precipice of taking some action that will lead to a change, I urge you to banish the excuses.

Excuses like, I don't have enough time. Turn off the TV, get up earlier and make the time.

Excuses like, well, that's not going to work out for me because things like that don't happen to people like me. Why not you?

Why not now? We all have the same opportunities as each other. Some people are simply better at creating new opportunities than others. But we all start somewhere.

And then there are the fear-based excuses.

What if I don't know the outcome?

What if they laugh at me for trying?

What if I make a start and then don't like it?

For each of the above and many more besides, you have to banish the 'what ifs'. Because these are simply fear based excuses for not taking action and not making a start to get that thing done.

Looking at the above, do any of us really know how things will pan out? What we can do is have a lot of fun on the journey finding out.

So please banish the 'what ifs', and if you find yourself thinking *what if it's going to go wrong...* Pause, take a breath, and reframe it so that you instead start thinking in terms of:

What if me getting visible leads to new opportunities?

What if I approach a journalist and they want to feature me?

In short, turn all your concerns into positives, so that you feel more fired up about getting started.

But if you don't take that initial leap of faith, how are you going to be able to put yourself out there to effectively say, I want this to be my reality as I know I can help so many other people along the way?

Whenever you have a wobble about starting something, and let's face it, we're all human, think about that all-important Why.

Before my real journey began, I made a pledge with myself that I was going to use my maternity time to write a book. I reasoned that there could be no more excuses. I'd always wanted to write one but had never quite found the time to do it. At the time, I was thinking of a fictional book aimed at young women and mums, but after J stopped a little girl from crying at a swimming pool, through simply holding her hand and smiling, I realised I wanted to use that small act of kindness to help spread happiness through a children's book instead. So, one day during one of his naps, I sat and wrote *James and the Amazing Gift*. It wasn't called that at the time, but I had something down on my laptop and I felt good about it. And then I left it there for six months. Why? Well, I reasoned with myself I had no idea what to do next anyway and maybe it wasn't going to be anything after all. I hasten to point out this was before I went on the journey that I'm taking you on with this book. And in my defence, we all have to start somewhere. It was only after a conversation with a business coach at the time, when she said, "You've written a book? What are you going to do about it?" that I thought, do you know what, she's right.

So, I researched illustrators. I researched which publishing company I wanted to use to help me make my book-writing dream a reality and put everything into action. I even had a website made, and I blogged all the time about my journey and started to build an audience. I did all of this whilst working a very busy full-time job, which included international travel, and J was only two at the time. And then, in October 2016, I was able to invite book bloggers, journalists and my friends and family including J, along to the launch for *James and the Amazing Gift*.

But what if I'd left that story untold on my laptop? What if I hadn't put myself out there and become a *Huff Post UK* blogger, been featured in *Woman & Home* magazine and *Daily Mirror*? What if I'd not followed through on that long-held dream to always write a book?

You see, life is what you make it. Your life can be truly extraordinary, not just run of the mill, but only if you choose for this to be the case. Only if you step out of your own way, get out of your comfort zone, and make things happen.

And you will find that once you take that initial step in the right direction you start to gain momentum. Things start to happen, and other opportunities appear; sometimes things you never dreamt were possible.

Your hopes and your dreams deserve you to show up, to give them time to become a reality. If not now, then when?

Make a pledge with yourself. Today you will do one small thing that will mean you will make a start towards those visibility goals. You have already been intentional with where you want to be and by when. Now you just need to take action one step at a time. And who knows where you will be in a week, a month, a year from now?

I've created a FREE Goal Setting workbook to help you get crystal clear on both your Business Objectives and your Communications Objectives so you know where you're heading and when you would ideally like to get there. **You can download it by visiting:**

www.njrpr.com/book

5

STORYTELLING, NOT SELLING

I have lost count of the number of people that I've worked with who really try to fight against the fact that the PR should be about them. They're highly successful business owners, or they're about to start or launch a new company, but when it comes to stepping into the limelight themselves, they question whether they can hide behind a product, the company, the service that they're offering, as that's their comfort zone. But PR should always be about you as the business owner. And the reason for this is that people buy from people. People want to know who you are, what you do and what your expertise is. They also want to understand how you managed to get to where you are today, but most of all, how you can help them.

Whether you like it or not, as uncomfortable as it may feel, if you want your company to be successful in this day and age, you must lead from the front, not try to blend into the background and hide away. In short, you need to tell your story.

When it comes to storytelling and not selling, this tends to be a real block for entrepreneurs because you naturally want to talk about your latest launch or product or whatever else it is that you're doing right now. But when was the last time that you opened a magazine or a newspaper and saw a massive puff piece all around Jennifer's new course, Zara's new membership or Dipti's new podcast? It rarely happens. Because everything is wrapped up in a story. So yes, it is possible to mention that shiny new podcast, but as part of a wider piece that highlights your story or an element of it.

Think about the last time you went out with friends and enjoyed some drinks and food. What, aside from a potential sore head the next day, do you remember most from that night? The anecdotes, the stories, the moments your friends told you about. Ever since we evolved, we have been sharing stories. It's one of the key fundamental pillars that makes us human.

It's also why storytelling is so powerful. It can change someone's perception or view of you instantly. It allows them to see how you can help them and through sharing your story, you're able to resonate with them on their own level.

When you think about stories, think about the kinds of things that you like to read, watch, or listen to. Things that are uplifting, showcasing a journey such as someone who's gone from being in debt to now being hugely successful, but with a few twists along the way, like Lisa Johnson, or someone that's defied the odds, and overcome something that's seemed insurmountable, like Meera Naran (you will read more about Meera later in this book). Those are the kind of stories that appeal to journalists and editors and it's what their readers/listeners/ viewers love to hear about. You may well believe that journalists are always on the look-out for negative news, but it's not true. Journalists are looking for inspiring, uplifting stories. Sometimes, these stories can be linked to the news agenda of the day or highlight something that a celebrity has done. Sometimes, it can simply be the telling of a special story, just like yours.

* * *

PR case study

The UK's first Drive-in Wedding

In October 2020, I worked on a story that went viral globally and was shortlisted for and subsequently went on to win PR awards. Saheli Mirpuri from Saheli Events came to me as she was working on an unusual wedding and wanted to know whether it would be newsworthy. When I looked at the elements of the story in front of me, I knew it could work well for the media, but it needed to be positioned as a UK first (another thing that news outlets like).

The story was this. It was the height of lockdown in the UK and couples could only get married in front of fifteen guests. It meant that the wedding industry at the time was on its knees. Gone were the days of having three-hundred-plus guests at lavish celebrations and big events. The only venues having success were the ones catering for smaller celebrations. But even then, with the chopping and changing of the rules, they too were struggling. Saheli's couple wanted to be married in front of all their friends and family. The question was, could they stage a drive-in wedding to make it all work?

Once a press release was written, I sold it into the national media and, working alongside a respected UK newswire, released the story everywhere. On the Tuesday, the story was featured across two pages of *The Times*.

It showed the couple celebrating and a view of the field next to the wedding venue with the cars parked up whilst the guests watched the wedding on a big screen. Entertainment and food were provided by masked waiters travelling from vehicle to vehicle on segue ways. Most importantly everything was COVID compliant because we were at the height of the pandemic. Right now, the media is feeding off the media like never before and when a story appears in one place, it can then be featured elsewhere. By lunchtime, the story had gone viral, appearing in *Mail Online*, on *ITV News, BBC News, BBC Radio Five Live*, and the majority of national newspapers ran the story online as the popularity and shareability of it grew. It meant my client was in great demand. She was being interviewed by *Channel Five News*, *BBC Radio 2* and international requests were also coming in. By the following day, the story had made the front page of *The Guardian*, but there was a point when she said to me, "Nicola, can I give these interviews to someone else on my team to complete because I'm so busy doing other things in my business? I need to do the client calls, and I need to look after other clients." My answer was no. Because you are your business. And as the spokesperson for your business, you need to be the one to be seen and the one to be heard. The business is named after Saheli, so it was important that she was the only person completing the interviews. By completing all the interviews (and in fairness, it was relentless for those first forty-eight hours) it helped position her as the expert in the luxury wedding events industry. She was in great demand as the person to speak to, especially as the couple in question completed one interview for the news wire for me, and then decided they didn't want to complete any more. You can't blame them, not when a journalist tracked them down and knocked on their front door and wouldn't go away. As with everything, the more your ideal clients see your name appearing in the media, the more likely it is that they will check out your website. And that's exactly what they did.

The reason that this story worked so well for the media is that it was uplifting at a time when people needed to see a snapshot of normality. It also gave people hope that there was a way forward. Here was an idea that could be replicated in such a way that it could help other brides and grooms who didn't want to have a smaller wedding but wanted to have all their loved ones present to see them get married.

So, yes, going back to my original point, any PR should always be about you as the founder of your business. And this works if you have a collaboration that you're doing with a celebrity or an influencer, and it works if you're releasing a creative news story. You should always be the one that is quoted and your company name or what you do should be featured in any piece too. Think about some of the big companies and brands that have successfully harnessed the power of PR. Virgin – Richard Branson. Apple – the late Steve Jobs. Microsoft – Sir Bill Gates. I know you think you're only just starting out and these guys are in the big league, but there's never any harm with starting as you mean to go on. Own the narrative of your company – it will pay dividends in the end. You are also missing a trick if you don't get your company mentioned – your ideal clients need to be able to find you, after all.

The first PR campaign I worked on was for Channel 4, to help raise awareness of their live Honda sky diving advert. Honda wanted to have a team of skydivers jumping out of a plane during an extended ad break, live on national TV, whilst spelling out the brand's name. Under the expert tutelage of my Account Director and one of the Managing Partners at the agency I was working at, we focused on highlighting the fact the event was going to happen. Armed with images from a test run, we approached all the national media, especially the picture desks, and told them the date and time that the actual jump would be made live on Channel 4. As a result, we secured coverage across the board in most of the national newspapers. And then, when the Honda team did successfully spell out the word in the allocated time, we had a second bite at the proverbial cherry – using the updated images to highlight what an amazing feat it had been.

The reason I'm highlighting this, is because it's a great lesson for you in knowing that any story you release or talk about needs to have a news hook and a reason for a journalist / publication to run it at that moment in time. Often, as business owners, we think that having a strong enough story is everything. And at times it can be. But if you can find an awareness day, week or month or a reason that something should run at a specific time of year, it is much more likely not to be squeezed by another story. In short, it can help ensure you some PR success, although of course, there are never any guarantees.

HOW TO DEEPER CONNECT WITH YOUR AUDIENCE

The more your ideal clients find out about you, the more you let them into your world, the more likely it is they will want to work with you. Loyalty is built from trust. There is nothing more powerful for you as a business owner than to be able to cement the know, like, and trust factor.

This is when someone finds out about what you do, they follow you and see what you're up to, and when they realise, you're the expert in your field and are genuine and authentic, they come to you to see if you can solve the problem that they have.

Nothing gives you this credibility more than telling your story.

Stepping out of your comfort zone and letting people know who you are and the journey you have been on can also be incredibly empowering for you too. And if it's handled correctly, and you are working with the right journalist (who respects that there is a person behind the headline and handles things sensitively), the resulting piece of coverage can be a game-changer.

This is why you need to do your research about the type of media you would like to be featured in. It's also worth looking at the journalists who are writing for those publications. Follow them on Twitter and Instagram and see what they're up to. Take the time to make a genuine connection with them. Perhaps they have just bought a new puppy and you also have a dog; perhaps they took up knitting during lockdown and you are heavily into crafting. Whatever it is, reach out and get to know them a bit better before you launch into giving them your story on an exclusive basis. It's important that you feel safe with whoever you tell your story to. Not so that you can tell them everything (remember to only share the things you want to share), but so that you know you're in the best possible hands.

Once your story is in the media – and especially if it appears online – it's there for good, so please get it right. You have worked hard to get your business off the ground, now you need to ensure that how you position your business, you as the founder and the brand, is exactly how you want it to be.

This is also why knowing all the angles to your story is so important. In a moment, I'll provide you with an exercise that will help you to start thinking about your story, but remember, your story also needs writing. So, even if you have a list of things or events that could make it into your story, I'd still suggest getting someone to write it for you. After all, it's harder to look at things objectively, especially when you're so close to the moments and events that happened.

I want you to know that I completely get how scary it is to start sharing your story.

To promote this book, I'm in the process of doing just that. I'm approaching journalists with my story and having highlighted many of the things that have happened. I'm also suggesting angles that could make (what I think are) interesting pieces.

In the past, I've been featured in *The Daily Telegraph*, talking about how I wished I'd been fitter and healthier when I had Covid back in March 2020. That led to me being interviewed on *LBC* and *BBC Radio Five Live* (which I also used as an opportunity to promote my children's book at the time, as it was just two weeks before it was published). I've also been filmed and featured on ITV's evening news talking about J K Rowling releasing her *Ickabog* story online (again, one week before my own book's publication).

In the next chapter, I'll tell you more about my journey as a children's author and how getting visible through PR not only helped to catapult me into mainstream media – but also opened lots of doors to incredible opportunities and it can do the same for you too.

Remember though, everything begins with your story. You are unique and no one else will have been through the same experiences as you. It's gold dust. Use it well and use it in a way that will help reach others, so you can impart your knowledge and your expertise, and grow that trust factor so you, in turn, have a loyal audience who want to hear what you have to say.

Start by providing expert tips and comments, if that feels more comfortable, before you progress to sharing your story or elements of it. But please don't hide as you would rather not be seen.

Those that adopt this approach in this day and age, unless they have already built up a previously loyal audience, are likely to come unstuck. Share your story and become known as someone who is the expert in your field by the media. And if you're still asking why, you should do this, just think about the opportunities that could come your way if you do.

I've had clients who have been featured and journalists have then come to me, further down the line, asking to speak to them again about their expertise. If journalists know you're reliable and professional, they will seek you out. But first, they have to know who you are, what you do, and how you can help others.

THE ANGLES OF YOUR STORY EXERCISE

Get yourself a blank piece of paper and on it, circle a big ME in the middle.

Then use a spider diagram with subject headings such as:

- Hobbies
- Health
- Relationships
- Points of difference
- Experiences

Then start to list out the things under each of these headings.

Perhaps you're a hula hoop champion but you haven't previously told anyone about it, perhaps you keep bees at the bottom of your garden because you understand their importance in our eco system, or perhaps you have a love for all things speed related and you're in your sixties. Whatever it is, write it down. It might not seem significant right now, but it could spark some ideas of an angle that you could approach a journalist with.

When it comes to your health, have you been on a journey? Are you suffering from a chronic incurable disease? Are you blighted by an unknown disability about which you haven't previously talked? These could all be relevant and interesting to journalists, but only if you're happy to share the details.

When it comes to relationships, think about incredible coincidences, friendships, things that have bonded you, any hurdles that you have overcome. Were you married on an unusual day? Did your partner propose several times before you said yes? Did you meet your soulmate in the most unusual but amazing way?

An important caveat to mention here is that if any angles of your story include someone else, please check with them in advance if they're happy to be featured in the media.

For instance, I know that my husband doesn't want to be interviewed and is very private, so I would never mention him in any interviews. He is usually referred to as a relative rather than who he is. But your partner may well be happy to be photographed alongside you or to talk about what you do and how it has impacted them and your relationship. This is important as you really can't agree to be interviewed, only for that person to cause problems further down the line and the piece has to be pulled. Always get agreement – in writing, if you can, and yes, that can be in an email, so it doesn't need to be a formal document as such.

For your points of difference, have a think about what makes you unique. Where do you work? Did you start your business, for instance, from the shed at the bottom of your garden but now you have a factory and a fully-fledged production line for the products in your business? Did you once meet someone who changed your life? Even better if it was a celebrity and they imparted some wisdom, and it has helped you go on and create a successful six-figure business.

Experiences should be an easy one for you to brainstorm. Think about things that have happened throughout your life. Perhaps you have been to some unusual places or something incredible has happened to you. As a rule of thumb, it's best to think about the last ten years rather than going much further back, but if something happened to you that was so significant, it's worth mentioning that too. For now, though, add it to the list so that you end up with a diagram that looks like the one opposite. It's a great starting point for pulling together all the angles of your story.

To help you further, I've created a FREE Storytelling not Selling workbook to help you really think about the angles of your story. **You can download it by visiting:**

www.njrpr.com/book

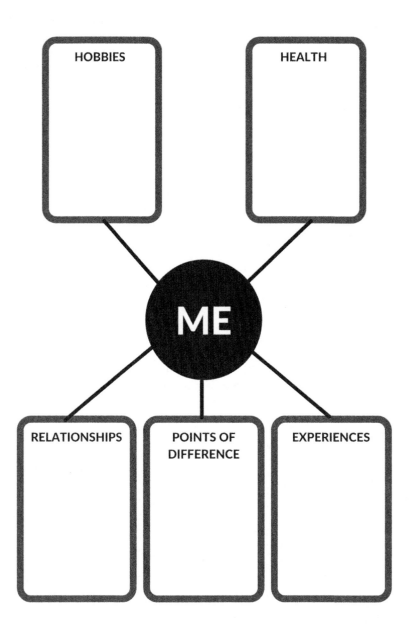

6

FACING THE FEAR

In November 2016, I was about to self-publish my first children's picture book and whilst I knew it would benefit from lots of awareness thanks to PR, for some reason, I was hesitating. I thought that despite already having eight years' experience in PR, it wasn't enough and that I needed to work with a book specialist. So, I searched for a suitable PR and found someone who was great but didn't really have any book PR experience. I paid out thousands of pounds and didn't really get much of a return. That's when I decided, I needed to give myself a stern talking to. I had poured my heart and soul into the book. My dad, who had been ill for a long time, had not long passed away and I needed something to take my mind off the emptiness I was feeling with his passing. So, I sat down and approached it how I approach all PR. I looked at the angles contained in the story, and I made a list of which publications I wanted to be seen in. Then, I thought about the contacts I had at each of those places and began to reach out to them.

What I found was, and I hope you will find this too, once I had success in one place, things started to shift and happen. I became a *Huff Post UK* blogger, I was featured in *Woman and Home* magazine, and a lovely piece followed in the *Daily Mirror,* and then *BBC Surrey* and *The Surrey Herald.* It was quite literally a snowball effect. And in an extensive blogger outreach programme – I started to make in-roads with mummy bloggers who posted and reviewed the book. I also approached celebrities that I knew or had worked with in the past, and soon the likes of Sara Cox, Amanda Lamb, Gemma Oaten, Anita Dobson, Michelle Heaton and Dr Ranj were talking about it. The more I talked about it, the more I raised awareness. I was also able to book school visits and sell up to sixty copies at a time. It helped spread the word massively and before I knew it, there I was standing in my local branch of Waterstones, completing not one, but two author book-signings and outselling the latest David Walliams release, two to one, on the day.

So, when it comes to putting yourself out there in terms of PR, I completely get how scary it can feel. What if no one likes what you have to say? What if they think you're showing off? What if it backfires and you don't like the piece, or you're quoted out of context?

The thing is, there are a million reasons why you can say you don't want to get started with PR, but I'm hoping that as you now have this book in your hands and you have made it this far, you're realising how many other people's lives you can impact and how you can now help them.

WORKING ON YOUR SELF BELIEF, CONFIDENCE AND GAINING CLARITY

What I'd like you to do is have a think about what is blocking you from getting started with PR.

Perhaps you don't feel confident in yourself. Perhaps there's a lack of belief around what you can do and achieve. Perhaps you don't feel worthy enough of success. Whatever it is, have a look at it. That feeling you get when someone says, 'I saw this opportunity that would be perfect for you, and you should go for it.' And yet for some unknown reason, you still hold yourself back. This is a form of self-sabotage as you are sabotaging an opportunity that has come your way and you're turning it down because of fear and the dreaded 'what ifs'.

Right now, if someone were to say to you, 'Would you like to be more visible?' chances are you would say yes. And yet, when it comes to being visible, for whatever reason, especially as a female entrepreneur, it can feel like the scariest thing in the world to put ourselves out there. It can feel like the most difficult thing we've ever done. So, I'd like you to work on your self-belief because in turn, this will impact your confidence. Coupled with having clarity around what you want to say, this will also give you a big boost, especially when it comes to approaching the media and being featured.

Remember that when you're approaching journalists, you're doing so on the basis that you're an expert in your field. But if, for whatever reason you don't feel like an expert, and you don't portray yourself as an expert, then guess what? You won't come across as an expert and they're unlikely to feature you. We talked in Chapter Three about the useful things to have in place before you even make PR approaches, i.e., professional pictures, having a good website, etc. (and remember, it doesn't matter if it's just a good landing page but the media like to have something that they can direct their readers to).

Let me ask you this: How do you feel about yourself, right now, on a scale of one to ten? How do you think you could get to that next level in your business and start attracting more clients? By hiding or by showing up and being visible so everyone knows who you are and how you can help them? Once you secure that first piece of PR, everything changes. I've seen it so many times, especially from the ladies in my PR Mastery Membership. Once that first piece lands, they become new business owners overnight as the self-belief just grows.

Do you already have paying clients? If so, then ask those paying clients what they think of your services. Feedback is a great way to improve and enhance your customer care. It also means that when people are contacting you and requesting your services, you can share with them the testimonials that you already have. It's worth also asking any potential new clients how they found you and what has led them to find out more about you. It will give you more of a picture about how your clients are discovering you.

If you're running a successful business, your clients should hopefully say lovely, positive things about you and tell you how you have helped them solve their problems and how you genuinely care.

What I'd love you to do, if you're feeling unsure of yourself or are not overly confident right now, is to go and buy yourself some post it notes. Once you have these, write out some of the positive things that your clients have said about you and display them somewhere you can see them every day. That way, when you're having a moment and you're thinking, I don't know that I can do this, you can remind yourself of the impact that you have already had on other people's lives, and how your clients currently feel about you. In doing this, you're changing your subconscious programming so you start to believe that you CAN do this, and you ARE an expert in your field.

Another thing I'd like you to do if you're struggling with your self-belief, is to write a personal statement. This will take you from where you are now to where you want to be in relation to PR (but it can also work for any area of your life too). So, for example,

I'm a successful business owner who has been featured in numerous national publications such as x, y, z (list them out here).

Say this affirmation/personal statement to yourself at least once a day. The more you do this, the more you will feel worthy to be able to achieve these results and the more you will be able to start believing that you can do this and you're going to get visible.

Having clarity around what you want to say, i.e., your key messages, or what you want to get across in any interview with any journalist will also help with this (go back and have a look at Chapter Two where we covered this in more detail). Why will it help? Being prepared will make you feel more in control of what you're going to say, and you will come across as knowledgeable and the true expert that you want to be.

When you're quoted in a magazine or a newspaper and someone else is reading it and thinking, 'What I really need right now is a hand with this issue I have going on in my life,' and then they see your name and website, who do you think they're going to contact?

How many times have you thought about buying something and

then you see the same thing over and over wherever you go? This happened to me a few months ago. I'd just agreed to purchase a new car in metallic dark blue, which is not what I thought I would go for, but what the dealer had available. As soon as I'd made that decision, how many other deep metallic blue cars do you think I saw? Everywhere I went, I kept seeing metallic dark blue cars whereas before, I'd seen none! When I was thinking about buying a white car – all I saw for a couple of weeks afterwards was white cars.

With securing PR, you need to know you absolutely can achieve results. Half the battle is making a non-negotiable agreement with yourself that you will make the time to prioritise taking consistent action and will not hold yourself back. Because if you hold yourself back, you're keeping your gift (what you do in your business) away from those who need it most.

IT'S ALWAYS ABOUT THEM AND NOT YOU

I mentioned this in the introduction to the book, but when it comes to your ideal clients and the ones you can help the most, PR is about raising awareness so you can help them. In short, it's not about you, it's about them. It sounds like an odd thing to say, but when it comes to PR and sharing your story, you're looking to, yes, raise your profile, yes, raise awareness, and position yourself as the expert in your field, but it's so that you can help them with that problem or issue that they have, or that they need solving.

What happened to me after I'd had J is that I didn't want to return to work full-time because I was struggling with separation anxiety, and in struggling with separation anxiety I felt alone. Separation Anxiety is a medically accepted form of mental illness. And when you have acute separation anxiety, you struggle with being apart from that person. From my perspective, if I had read an article in a magazine or a newspaper from someone who was talking about how they could help working mums park the mum guilt or find a way to feel better about going back into the workplace, so they didn't feel awful 24/7, that would have made things so much easier for me. When you read a magazine piece or see a news report that resonates with you in this way, you feel like you're not alone and you're not going through things by yourself. So, using PR as a vehicle to reach your ideal clients and let them know what you do, can quite literally help someone just like me, who used to sit in the toilet cubicle at work crying because she missed her child, but had also lost her own identity since becoming a mum. Surely that's an amazing gift that you can give to that person. That is why what you do, and the journey that you have been on, and the experiences that you have had, deserve to be talked about in the media. Perhaps you can impact the life of someone who has just lost a child, maybe you can impact someone who really needs to get on top of their stress and anxiety. Hearing from you as an expert can help them see there is hope and light at the end of the tunnel.

Hopefully, you can now see how, through sharing what you do, you can have a massive impact on others. Please don't hide because you think you don't have a big purpose-filled message to share. Products or the service that you offer can often speak volumes themselves. Remember, people buy from people. And if people resonate with your story and they understand where you're coming from, they're going to want to work with you, follow you and they could become early adopters and then they go on to become your most loyal customers.

When people understand your story and where you have come from, they naturally resonate with you on a much deeper level.

They understand where you're coming from. There's something special in that. So no, it's never about you. Please go and park your ego and the 'what ifs' and the 'I'm not sure I'm quite ready for this yet.' Because if not now, then when? Those ideal clients looking for someone to help them need you now – not next week, or next year, when all your ducks are in a row and your branding has been relaunched. Now it's up to you to go on and impact more people and more lives through what you do.

7

APPROACHING JOURNALISTS

As small business owners, journalists can seem like they're untouchable. You can't speak to them, and you can't reach out to them. And when you do, they don't come back to you anyway. We know that they're busy, but we also question why they would want to speak to us. But I'm telling you from the perspective of someone who was a journalist for thirteen years and now works in PR, journalists are always looking for great stories. If you have a great story, they really do want to hear from you. Please don't hold back because you have a notion that they're too busy to find the time to speak to you. It's just not the case.

Yes, they are very busy, and, in some cases, they receive five hundred emails a day. Stop for a moment and think about what your inbox would look like if you received that many emails. Bearing this in mind, the absolute key is to make your email count and stand out. Think about the subject line that you use. Make it as interesting as possible, so that it appeals. When you write the email, make it short and sweet. Three paragraphs are ideal, stating what it is that you do, how you can help them, and a line or two about your expertise and the angles of your story you can talk about. Quite often, a journalist will have thirty seconds to a minute to be able to scan through your email. They might not be able to read everything you say, so please don't attach lengthy media biographies or lots of attachments, as they just won't have the time to look at them.

Instead, use bullet points to highlight the areas you could talk about and the angles in your story that might be of interest. And think about where in the publication it could work. Is there a particular feature or something you have seen that has recently run and could help move the story forward? All of this will help set you apart from other business owners who are also looking to secure publicity. If you see a journalist post a request on, say, Twitter with the hashtag #journorequest, message straight away. If they provide an email address or say their DMs (direct messages) are open, contact them immediately that way.

But please pay attention to exactly what they're looking for. If you're not a great fit for this opportunity, please don't respond with something spurious that you hope might fit. Put yourself in the journalist's shoes. If you're on a tight deadline, there's nothing worse asking for one thing, and getting responses that are neither relevant nor useful to what you're looking for. If for instance you're a florist specialising in weddings, but the journalist is looking for someone who has specifically started knitting recently, not surprisingly flower arranging isn't going to fit with what they're after. I know it seems like the most obvious thing to say and it really should be, but you would be surprised at how many PRs even get this wrong.

Please don't try and respond with your own agenda or mention something completely different to them when they're probably on a tight deadline from their editor. They're trying to gather as much information as they can within a very short space of time, and they want to get the feature written and sorted as soon as possible. With this in mind, when it comes to contacting journalists, if you do reach out to someone and they come back to you, please don't just leave that response in your email for a few days and think you might go back at some point when you're less busy because you know the dog needed walking or you had a quick client call or whatever else. Make sure you respond professionally and promptly, asking when their deadline is so that you know when you need to respond to their request in a timely manner.

In a moment we're going to come on to what journalists do and don't want. As part of this, responding straight away to a request, is important. The more professional, reliable, and helpful you are, the more they will come back to you for a comment again. Be the person that makes it into their contact book, not the one that has a mark against your name saying #unreliable. If journalists know they can rely on you and you're an expert in your field, they will come back to you. I know this works because I've had several people in my membership who have had this happen. The more that you put yourself out there, the more you talk about what you do, the more likely journalists looking for an expert in your field are going to find you. If you then make yourself available and answer their questions straight away, they are going to come back to you again and again.

The other thing that will really work in your favour is to always check when a journalist's deadline is. That way you can work towards meeting it. It's worth noting that journalists are a bit like elephants in that they have long memories, and they remember the people that have let them down at the last minute. If you get featured somewhere, whether it's on radio, TV, print, online or a publication runs your piece, always send a quick thank you email. It really does go a long way. How many times have you done something for someone else and if they don't say thank you, you feel a bit miffed? Whereas if you say thank you to a journalist, they do remember it. Politeness costs nothing.

The other thing to mention is to never badger a journalist for a response. If they don't reply, they might just be busy. Don't take it personally. It's very easy to sit there thinking, 'Oh gosh, what is it that I've done or what didn't work with that?' If they're interested, nine times out of ten, they will come back quickly, unless of course, they're busy doing another feature, or they're on deadline elsewhere. And then a few days could pass. If you still haven't heard from them, it's okay to follow up once politely saying something along the following lines.

I was just wondering whether you saw this and if it's of interest to you?

If they still don't respond, you have to accept that on this occasion it hasn't worked. It doesn't mean you can't approach them on another day with another story. It's always about finding the angles that are going to work for them within the timeframe that they're working towards. We've looked at ignoring messages or emails for hours on end, but I've had so many cases where people have come to me saying they responded to a request on Twitter but then forgot to check in again, and the deadline for the piece has now expired. This is a good example of a wasted or missed opportunity.

Never, ever miss a deadline. If you miss a deadline in terms of getting your written quotes or comments back to the journalist, they are well within their right to move on and give that opportunity to someone else.

We talked earlier about the importance of images, and I can't stress enough that you should never make the mistake of thinking that images don't matter. They're hugely important, especially when it comes to telling your own story, and it can be the difference between something running or not. If you don't have professional images or collects to accompany something, be prepared that your story might not get published.

Another thing you need to not do is approach a journalist without looking at the publication they work for and working out where your story could be featured. You will be surprised how many business owners and PRs also do this. They don't get hold of the magazines, they don't listen to the podcast episodes, they don't listen to the radio or watch the TV programme in question before they blindly say, I'd like to be featured. Why should they feature you? Where should they feature you? Is there enough of a hook for your story, i.e., is there a reason they should be running something at a certain point in time? Really think about these elements because it's important if you want to be successful with PR.

Journalists tend to fall into one of two camps. Some say don't attach anything at all as they don't want their inboxes clogged up; others say, please attach a picture of yourself. There is no right or wrong way to approach this. From what I can tell, magazine journalists prefer to see who is emailing them so like a picture attached, but when it comes to national newspapers or their associated online sites, unless they specifically ask for something, don't attach it.

The other thing to not do is send them a link to your latest blog post and expect them to trawl through it to find the information they're looking for. Remember they tend to only scan emails for thirty seconds to one minute. Put yourself in a journalist's shoes and look at things from their perspective.

If a journalist comes back to you and asks for you to attach a professional picture of yourself, make sure it's not a huge file size which is going to clog up their inbox. Also, make sure that once you have completed an interview, if it's about an element of your personal story, always ask for a read back. This is where the journalist will usually call you and read back the copy they're planning to submit to their editor. They might not always be able to give you one because it might be against the editorial policy of the publication, but it's always worth asking – at least you will have tried. And if you are given a read back, please ensure you give it your full attention. Don't arrange the phone call when you have lots of distractions. If need be, go and sit in your car for some quiet whilst you listen back to the piece. This is your final chance to check that you're fully happy with it before it's published.

Always ask for a credit for your website and to be introduced doing whatever it is you do in your business. If you're a florist for instance, and your name is Kate James, you want the piece to mention florist Kate James, who runs Iris Flowers in Beaverton, by way of an introduction and then to have your website at the bottom of the piece. This is so that people who are interested in what you do and who you are can find you. Remember that trail of breadcrumbs.

If you're writing a piece for journalists, make sure you provide them with a pre-written introduction of a couple of lines that outlines what the piece is about. And then, at the bottom, you can put more details about you and your website link.

I briefly mentioned subject lines earlier, but I can't stress enough about the storytelling, not selling element here. No journalist in their right mind (unless they're just writing about your business for a targeted feature) will click on an email that is clearly just selling something. **Exclusive case study**

works well, and I follow it up with a bit of detail about the story. Think of things in terms of headlines. If you can't sum up your story in a headline, how will the journalist be able to do this too? If you're proactively going to a journalist, and saying, 'Are you interested in my story?' they may well have to go to either a commissioning editor or an editor of the magazine, and say, 'What do you think about this?' and they will need to sum it up in one line. It comes down to being helpful again. And of course, editorial decisions rest with the editor of that publication or programme. You can't force anyone to run something just because you think it should run. That's the beauty of earned media – it is infinitely more valuable as a result, rather than it being an advertorial or advertising.

Strong, well thought out opinion pieces that work well for their specific publication are also great, and another great email subject can be

Publication name: Exclusive - My Journey from A to B

When it comes to reactive media requests, i.e., the ones where the journalist has said they're actively looking for experts to feature, it's always worth responding with the subject line referring to what the request is about.

For instance, if a journalist is looking for exclusive case studies of women who have overcome trauma or addiction, a good subject line would be:

Exclusive Case Study – Trauma / Addiction – Tessa Greenhatch

As a recap, here is what journalists do and don't want:

WHAT JOURNALISTS WANT

- Good, reliable case studies with strong stories
- Professional approaches
- Business owners who have great images to accompany their stories
- A short succinct email that sums up the story in a few paragraphs
- An easy-to-read subject line that is about storytelling, not selling
- Someone who meets the deadlines they're working to
- Exclusive case studies (it makes them look good to their editor)

WHAT JOURNALISTS DON'T WANT

- Unreliable case studies who pull out of interviews at the last minute
- Lengthy emails that ramble (they're likely to get deleted)
- Attachments that clog up their inbox or lengthy media bios
- Emails that ask them to look at links to content (they don't have time to read it)
- No images to highlight the story
- People that miss deadlines
- Responses to a request that don't relate to that request

- Interviewees who change their mind at the last minute about being featured
- Interviewees who haven't checked whether someone else involved in their story can be included

Don't just take it from me though. Here are some thoughts from journalists about what they look for and the kind of things that do and don't work for them.

"If I don't come back to you straight away, it's usually because I haven't seen your email. I try really hard to respond, but I get a lot of emails and so if I don't reply after a few weeks, please follow up once again. As we're monthly publications, things do get held onto for quite some time, so I squirrel things away and then, when it comes to a certain theme I may well be back in touch. So, if it's a no in the first instance, please remember it may not be a no forever."

— ELLA DOVE, COMMISSIONING EDITOR *RED, GOOD HOUSEKEEPING* AND *PRIMA*

"Be upfront with a journalist from the off. Ask at the outset can they mention your business, include a URL etc. Better to get that all sorted before either of you spend any time on a feature. And be flexible: sometimes a URL cannot run in print, but it can run on the online version."

— EIMEAR O'HAGAN, FREELANCE JOURNALIST, TWITTER: @EIMEARFREELANCE

"As a freelance journalist writing for the nationals, the first thing I look for in a pitch is whether it's an exclusive, whether the story has run elsewhere or whether it's been pitched to other journalists.

It's always better for me to pitch an exclusive that hasn't already been sent to other staff journalists as, if it's been rejected by a news desk, that publication isn't then going to pay me to write the story for them. Pitches from PRs or business owners need to make this clear.

I then look at the 'top lines' - what makes this person's story stand out from the rest? Is it topical? Does it have a good hook? Have I read similar before? So, a pitch needs to be clear and include a timeline of details.

Does the case study have good photos? Images are incredibly important. All publications like a case study-led story to have pictures that show what the story is about - so ones that have been taken across that timeline. Around 10-15 is good.

Lastly, can the case study be named? Only in very rare instances, usually for legal reasons, will a publication commission a story with an anonymous case study.

This is enough in the first instance for me to decide whether a pitch is one I can see being commissioned by national newspaper editors."

— CAROL DRIVER (WWW.MAKETHEHEADLINES.CO.UK/ WWW.CAROLDRIVER.COM)

THE POWER OF AN OPINION PIECE

Alongside other forms of earned media coverage, I am a huge fan of opinion pieces. Why? Because it gives you a chance to say how you really feel about a topic that's both newsworthy and relevant. Of course, the caveat here is that you don't want to be so polarising in your views that it damages your brand or business. But a well thought out opinion piece can really make a huge difference in highlighting a cause or something that is close to your heart, or something you feel others should know about.

Rather than me explaining the ins and outs of opinion pieces, I asked the Opinion Editor at *Metro*, Jess Austin to explain a typical day and to highlight any no no's when it comes to pitching. I first met Jess back in 2016 when she was working at The Huffington Post and she used to commission my features for the parenting and lifestyle sections as a blogger.

How does an average day look for you?

I get in at around 8am, catch up on emails and see which news stories may lend themselves to strong opinion and first-person takes. We have a morning conference at 9am for editors, followed by a meeting with my team where we discuss the pieces we have going out that day (usually around four articles that are a mix of series, evergreen first-person stories and timely reactions to news angles), ideas and what we want to commission. The rest of the day is spent juggling edits for pieces that have come in, finding the perfect writers for new ideas, commissioning, doing phone interviews, replying to pitches, and planning our on-going series and what to do to mark any dates of note in the coming weeks. I like to leave the day with a relatively formed schedule for what we'll be publishing the next day and we finish with a quick team meeting to talk through what we've done that day and if there are any outstanding issues.

What makes a compelling pitch for an opinion piece?

The most important thing for me is to know why an author is best placed to write the piece. I want to know about what makes them an expert on this issue and what examples they would bring into the piece to bolster their argument.

It's also great when a pitch includes at least three points that the author will make in the piece. I want to be certain what the author's opinion is and the conclusions they will draw - rather than have them ask lots of questions without solutions. I like to see the best lines near the top of the pitch; are there some shocking newsy stats? Is there one anecdote the author would like to share that is particularly striking? Aside from that, it's great to see any pictures that the author can provide as it saves us coming back to you to ask for them. However, we also need to know if we have the permission of the photographer to use them. Similarly, if pitching a sensitive piece - from a sexual assault survivor, for example - we need as much context as possible. Does the author have a conviction? Is the accused still alive? Can you provide a waiver from the author saying they consent to sharing their experience? One of my biggest no no's is when people pitch stories from people who are unable to write the pieces they are putting to us - usually for legal reasons.

Any definite no no's when business owners approach you?

On the back of the above, one of the biggest no no's is when businesses withhold information in the pitch. It's essential we know straight away any details that might impact us publishing the piece. For example, does the author need title sign off? Is it necessary that we include a mention of a brand? Does the author not want to share pictures of themselves? Does it need to go out on a certain day?

Another big no no is overt plugginess. If it's clear that the purpose of this piece is just a method of promoting the business - even if it's disguised well - it's not going to appeal to editors or readers. A big turn off when receiving pitches is when it's clear the person getting in touch has never read the section. That could be evident in them pitching something we have already published or suggesting an angle that does not fall under that section's remit.

Where do people go wrong when pitching to you?

It's not a definite no no, but my preference is not to receive a 'finished piece' in a pitch. I want to be sent an idea, which I can work with the author or PR to shape through a brief. It's far easier for us to start from scratch then retrospectively edit a finished piece. While with newsy angles, it's great to receive pitches that are ripe for same-day turnaround, with awareness days and weeks, it is better to send these ideas well in advance. Editors will have planned their content for these days - like Mental Health Awareness Week or International Women's Day - sometimes months in advance. Quite often, I get brilliant ideas from businesses and authors, but they come through the day before, by which point I've already commissioned all I'm going to on the topic.

CONSISTENCY

As with all things, when it comes to PR, consistency and consistently reaching out to journalists is key. You may well have heard other business owners say if you do things on a consistent basis, you will be seen more often. There's a reason for that. It's true. If you were to make three or four separate approaches of PR, every single week without fail, you are much more likely to end up securing some great pieces of coverage that will not only elevate you and your brand but will go on to help those ideal clients of yours too. Think about your message. Think about what you want the outcome of any piece of PR to be. And think about the impact you want that piece to have. There is no reason you can't do this. Journalists are just like you and me, except they're just super busy and they need business owners like yourself to be reliable, professional and on the ball.

WHAT TO SAY, WHAT TO DO AND HOW OFTEN

By now, I hope you have realised the importance of having clearly defined Business and Communications Objectives that align with each other. That way, you now know when in the year you need to be focusing on being more visible. I always advise my clients that a roller coaster of activity is best. By this, I mean sometimes you're focusing on securing PR through the media, and at other times, not so much so. This doesn't mean that you shouldn't continue with other forms of marketing in these quiet periods though. Make sure you're emailing your list every week. Ensure you consistently post across your chosen social media channels. And you should always be pursuing opportunities such as speaking gigs that are going to raise your profile. All these activities will help to elevate your expert status and your credibility. PR really can be the icing on the cake and the ultimate thing that will help you scale your business to another level and attract bigger brands to want to work with you.

We heard earlier from Lisa Johnson, how after a particularly good piece of PR, when she launched her podcast successfully, it led to her securing a traditional book deal. Always think of that trail of breadcrumbs. PR is a long-term strategic way of looking at things. Quick wins can and do happen but having a longer-term approach can serve you much better.

When it comes to climbing to the top of your business roller coaster and getting ready for a sustained period of PR activity, please bear in mind that journalists really do like exclusives. Think about the elements of your story and how they tie in with what you're looking to achieve. Are there specific stories you can pitch to different publications? Would an opinion piece work well to highlight how strongly you feel about something? Perhaps a guest post on a site such as *Huff Post UK* would work well (provided you have a strong enough news hook, that is). These could then be used in conjunction with well-placed tip-led and comment style pieces or features, showcasing your expertise. And then coupled with a well-placed piece that highlights an element of your story. All the above used in conjunction with each other would be incredibly impactful.

Add in your social media posts, highlighting what you're talking about, a profile-raising speaking opportunity, and you have yourself a well-rounded and successful PR campaign that will enhance how your ideal clients see both you and your business.

That's why it's so important to know the media and their deadlines, and why you need to be able to react to the news agenda, through what is known as news jacking, by being available to provide a comment around a current topic. The world of news works at an incredible speed. What makes headlines today, may not be the same as tomorrow. A big story though, will run and run and often includes things like a huge event such as the Olympics, political turmoil, a natural disaster or, as we have seen more recently, the pandemic.

It can feel incredibly frustrating to do all the above work, writing your story, knowing your key messages, refining your pitch, only to send an email and to not hear back. You can absolutely follow up once, but no more than that. Quite often I find that if a journalist is interested in something you have sent them, they're pretty quick to respond. Especially if it's an exclusive that you're offering.

Tenacity is everything when it comes to PR. You can't give up at the first hurdle as you just won't get anywhere. Instead, maybe you need to look at a different angle, try a different publication or approach another journalist. But please, whatever you do, don't badger anyone to respond to you. It's not smart, it's not kind and it's really not clever.

8

WHAT TO DO IN A CRISIS

I'm approached all the time by entrepreneurs and business owners who are, or feel they have been, misquoted. And it is this fear of being misquoted that has then put them off from ever getting visible through the power of PR again. It is a completely understandable fear. What you don't want to happen is that your story, or your brand which you have worked so hard to build, is portrayed in a light that you don't want it to be. However, if you follow all the steps in this book and you have your key messages in front of you, as well as being aware of what you want the outcome of any interview to be, the chances are that any piece of PR will reflect exactly what you have said.

I mentioned it earlier, but if you naturally over-share, and you say things that you later regret, you need to be aware that those comments are difficult to retract. When it comes to this, there has to be a point where the responsibility for over-sharing lies with you. My advice? Practise what you want to say beforehand. And if you are still worried about saying something you don't want out there, make yourself a note and have it in front of you, that says, do not say anything about x, y, or z. Now, I appreciate that this could work in completely the wrong way, in terms of, you might be the sort of person that has a note in front of you that says do not say anything about x, y or z and that makes you want to talk about it more, but at least you have tried to stop yourself from saying something negative.

Always think through how you want any interview with a journalist to go. It may well be that they will ask difficult questions. If there are questions, you're struggling to answer or you feel that they're trying to get you to say something you don't want to say, it's simple. Don't say it. You can always respond by saying, 'I'm really sorry, but I'd rather not comment on that.' This is perfectly fine, and it is much better in terms of safeguarding you, your business, and your brand than you saying something you later go on to regret. In the past, I've worked with celebrities, and they have over-shared or said something I'd much rather they hadn't. It was only through appealing to the good nature of the journalists concerned that those more damaging revelations did not end up in print. It is very difficult to take back something that you have already said, so don't say it. And if you are likely to say something negative, try and sit on it. Please only ever come out with something positive, otherwise you could end up becoming the story, but in a way that you hadn't envisaged or imagined.

I had an instance of a client who did a TV interview and she said one negative thing, and that one thing was the only part used. That's not a great way to reflect your brand, or for people to hear about you, which they're likely to be doing for the first time.

This is why I say it's never about responding to the first journalist request that you see. You have to think about any opportunity that you go for. Will it be good for your business? Will it enhance your reputation? Or could it be more damaging in the long term? No opportunity is worth it, and that's coming from me as a PR professional who would love you to secure as much coverage as possible. Brand reputation is everything.

If you are working in the cake industry, for instance, you do not want to be saying that all brides are bridezillas and fly off the handle at the drop of a hat, because who would want to book someone who makes a sweeping statement like that?

Really think about the kind of pieces that you respond to and the pieces that you end up securing for yourself. Will it end up being more hassle than it's worth? In terms of being quoted, and especially when it comes to your personal stories, I always recommend that you ask for a read back. This is where the journalist will either call you over the telephone after the interview and read back the whole piece or your quotes, so they know you're fully happy with the piece ahead of publication. Of course, it may well be against the policy of some publications to give you this read back, but if you have a poignant story and it's sensitive in its nature, I would ask for this right at the start of your dealings with the journalist so you know whether you want to pursue this opportunity or not. Never get to the stage where you have completed an interview and then you ask for a read back. By this point the journalist has every right to refuse, and it will be too late because they already have your story.

As part of any read back please also understand that you can't go through the piece and change everything. At the end of the day, when it comes to PR, securing editorial coverage for your business or your company is all about that all-important third-party endorsement, and there has to be a level of impartiality for the journalist / publication. Your quotes are likely to be part of a wider piece. You can't be trying to dictate the terms of how something comes across. So, again, it comes down to preparation and asking in advance, 'What is the angle that you're taking on this piece?' And if, at that stage, the journalist says, 'Oh we're going to be looking at this and this,' and that doesn't fit your agenda in terms of what you're doing, you can always ask how balanced the piece will be. This way you have a choice. You can either walk away if you don't like their answer or you can continue with the interview, knowing what angle the journalist and publication is going to take. If in doubt, always trust your intuition. If something doesn't feel right, it rarely is.

INACCURACIES AND WHAT TO DO ABOUT THEM

If you feel that there are inaccuracies in the piece when it gets printed or published, the most important thing for you to do is to look at where it's been printed, published, or broadcast. It's much harder when it comes to radio/TV to change what you have already said, as it will be your voice / face that people see. So, for the sake of this part, we'll be concentrating on stories appearing in print, online and in magazines. If you see something in print in a national newspaper and feel that it is inaccurate and unfair, nine times out of ten, it is likely to also appear online. Your number one priority at this stage is not to worry about the print piece, because that's much harder to change – unless of course you feel you need an apology. But the online piece is the most important to get corrected. Why? Because anything online, stays online and if something is incorrect there, more of your ideal clients are going to see that version, than they are likely to see a specific paper on a specific day. This is very much a rule of thumb, but in the first instance you want to go back to the journalist that you spoke to. Make sure that everything is in writing and politely (no matter how you're feeling) outline any inaccuracies. Thank them for their help with the story but point out that you feel there are some inaccuracies, and you would like these corrected as soon as possible. Then list out what is wrong. Do not send a great big rambling email about how annoyed or upset you are and everything else in between. You can say that you're upset, and bearing in mind the sensitive nature of the story, could these changes please be made as soon as possible?

Since the pandemic, it has been much harder to reach journalists because so many of them over the last couple of years have started working from home. With the nature of breaking news and competing priorities, it can also be difficult to get hold of even the journalist that you dealt with in the first place. But if you politely request any amends to be made in an email and you don't hear back from them, think if you have a telephone number from when they called you for the interview. If you're unsure of what to say or do, write it down in the email first and have that email in front of you before you start to call. You don't want to miss off any of the things that you would like to be changed. Please do not do the following: get irate and send a snappy email to them saying there are inaccuracies, followed by another one after you have re-read the piece pointing out further inaccuracies, and then a third email saying you have also spotted something else further down the piece.

Believe me, this does happen and who do you think the journalists are more likely to listen to? The polite email, with the points that need changing succinctly listed out, or the long, rambling, irate message from someone who then keeps emailing time and again throughout the day?

Most journalists are incredibly reasonable and if they've made an inadvertent mistake, they know they need to change it, and so they will. It is rarely through malice that this happens, so please don't convince yourself otherwise and swear that you will never speak to a journalist again.

Changes to pieces, especially online, do get made all the time. It might take a little bit of time, but any inaccuracies should be corrected. In very rare cases, you might find that the inaccuracies aren't changed, and you're sitting there, really concerned about the story, but you don't know what to do. So many people have come to me in the past and they haven't even approached the journalists to ask for the inaccuracy to be changed. But equally, they hadn't prepared in advance for their interview; they say they had no idea what angle the journalist was planning to take, or their words have been twisted and now they feel misrepresented. But can you see that if they had asked in advance about the angle of the story, whether it would be a balanced piece and if they could have a read back, how different the outcome would have been for them?

Instead, suddenly when their interview or story makes it into print, it's a bit of a shock, and then they're tearing their hair out saying, 'But that wasn't what was agreed and that wasn't what was said.' By this point though, it's your word against the journalist's and they are likely to have recorded your interview so they will have a back-up version of what was said. As you would do with your receipts for expenses, keep all your emails with journalists so you have a record of what's been said. If they say in this email train, this is going to be a piece about this and I'm going to look at this angle, and then the piece ends up being completely different, you may well have some redress but again, last minute editorial changes get made. An over-eager sub editor can write a headline to capture people's attention that may be detrimental to you, even if the journalist has been respectful, caring and trying to make sure this doesn't happen. What I would say at that point, if you're tearing your hair out as a small business owner, is seek help from someone that knows what they're doing in terms of crisis communications. That would be someone like myself, who's worked in PR for a long time and is used to working not only to get people into the media, but keeping brands, products, and businesses out of the media as well. I can't stress enough how important it is to get someone on board who knows what they're doing and how to find a way to be able to reach the editorial team, the journalists, the editor, if needs be. But you have to give them the full picture. It's no good saying one thing and then, 'Oh yes, well I kind of did say that though, really.' You have to be honest, and it's important that you do that straight away.

If, on any occasion, you're contacted by journalists because something has happened and it's involving your business, and a journalist says, 'I'm writing a piece about x, y or z and I'd like your comments on this,' what you need to ask is, 'Can I please check when your deadline is for this story? I will come back to you as soon as I can to meet that deadline with a comment or quote that you can use.' Please don't receive a phone call from a journalist or an email and then sit on it until two days later, because by that point the piece could already have run, and the journalists will be within their right to say, we contacted Bakes and Bees, but there was no comment. This can be more damaging in the long run for you than anything else. You have to find out the deadline and what's going on. And I'd argue that if you were contacted by journalists, asking for comment and you could see this could become a big issue for your business, get help:

Find someone who works in PR, who can help you with crisis comms and can step in for you and help you write a good state-ment which meets the journalist's deadline, and make sure that it reflects the position of your brand. Sometimes, you have to call in the experts; it's no good trying to do it all and weather the storm by yourself. The best handling of crisis communications is when you're honest and you're upfront. And if you have made a mistake, you hold your hands up and say so straight away. The stories that end up running for days on end are because someone doesn't do this right at the very beginning. If you're not sure what all the facts are, make sure you know everything that has happened and only then provide a comment to the media, not before. If it's a case that something's happened and you acknowledge this is the case, sometimes a simple, 'We're now investigating what has happened and will be looking at the lessons that can be learned from this' will suffice.

If you think about the scandals that have engulfed politicians or things that have damaged the reputation of businesses, you should be able to see where they have gone wrong.

Take jewellery firm Ratners for instance, and the PR gaffe made by the then founder Gerald Ratner in 1991, which wiped £500m off the value of the company, forcing stores to close and him to resign. At an Institute of Directors conference, he said his company sold a "crap" sherry decanter for £4.95 and joked that a prawn sandwich would last longer than a set of 99p earrings available at his stores. He also allowed himself to be photographed by a national newspaper with a gun pointed at his head following the furore about his comments, in an attempt to move on from the controversy. It's one of the biggest own-goal PR-gaffes but it highlights why you don't go down the road of negative comments to spark humour around your brand.

When you don't admit that something's happened, or you bury your head in the sand, that's when the story continues and becomes much bigger. In this instance, you don't want to fan the flames with comments that could escalate everything. It's not worth it. Sometimes things will happen but doing your best to limit the damage to your brand or business is key.

THE IMPORTANCE OF A CRISIS Q&A DOCUMENT

This is why I always think it's wise for you, as a business owner, to have a crisis question and answer document already written before you even begin doing any PR. What do I mean by this? This a document where you have sat and thought about all the things that could possibly go wrong in your business. It will be any issues that could cause people, or a complainant or a business partner to go to the media and say something about your company. For instance, perhaps you run a leisure venue and several people experience food poisoning from your restaurant and your customers have to go to hospital. It is highly likely that someone, especially in this age of citizen journalism, will go to the media or take it upon themselves to post a complaint on Twitter rather than coming directly to you as the business owner first. As journalists are always scrolling through Twitter for stories, they are likely to find it, unless you can reach that person in time and help them solve their grievance straight away, so they remove their comments. In short, you must be prepared for this.

Scenario one

You run a successful cake business and your business is doing well. You hand deliver one of your cakes to the venue ahead of a celebration. However, the couple that you deliver it to later take it upon themselves to try to add something extra to the cake. In doing so though, they make it not look as good as when it was delivered. They then take a picture of the damaged cake, post it on social media and say how disappointed they are with the service they have received from your business (tagging you in).

What I hope you will do is the following. Because you know that these things happen, you will have taken a photo of the cake in situ at the venue when it was delivered and have a timestamp on the image. That way, when you see the complaint, you can respond quickly and effectively to their tweet with your picture and that story is not likely to go anywhere.

Scenario two

You run a successful cake business and your business is doing well. You hand deliver one of your cakes to the venue ahead of a celebration. However, the couple that you deliver it to later take it upon themselves to try to add something extra to the cake. In doing so though, they make it not look as good as when it was delivered. They then take a picture of the damaged cake, post it on social media and say how disappointed they are with the service they have received from your business (tagging you in). You have been so busy on the day that you have forgotten to take a picture of the cake in situ at the venue and now it is your word against the couple's as to whether

the cake was indeed delivered in this way. You're also busy with deliveries so you don't look at your social media accounts until the following Tuesday, by which time, a local influential journalist has called to say they're thinking about running a story about how you ruined the couple's wedding day. At this point, I would contact the venue and get hold of the wedding planner who would be able to corroborate your version of events, to minimise any damage to your reputation.

In addition, I would then use some of your questions and answers from your crisis Q&A so that you can issue a statement along the lines of:

"We take great pride in every one of the cakes that we create. We work tirelessly to ensure that our clients are happy, and the cake in question was delivered at such and such a time to such and such venue. We are at a loss to understand how a cake that was delivered looking like this, ended up as it did and the wedding coordinator from (the venue) has agreed that when the cake arrived, it looked perfect. If my clients would like to discuss this with me, I'm more than happy to do so."

In this instance, it sounds as if someone is trying to actively ruin your reputation.

Stick to the facts and the truth. If it were to ever get to court, if you have proof on your side, then you will be fine. Journalists will usually also think twice about running stories if they think that legal action could be taken and what they have reported could be seen as inaccurate.

If, however, they have not checked their facts, and they have twisted something to make it look bad, you absolutely have grounds to ask for an apology as it's your reputation at stake. You also have grounds to ask for another story talking about the great cakes you make.

So, have a think about the kind of issues that could come up for you. Write out a Q&A document. Maybe you make products that are very bespoke, and are hand delivered to someone, and then someone says, 'That's not what I ordered,' or perhaps you work for a venue and there's a power cut and they complain that their special day/event has been ruined but it's outside of your control. With all these things you should always have a Q&A

written and, hopefully, also a contingency plan in case anything along these lines takes place.

The thing to remember is that you never comment to a journalist who rings you, pressing you for a response. You can give them a comment, but only after going away and thinking about it and checking their deadline by which time you need to respond.

BEING MISQUOTED

If you feel that you have been misquoted and it's damaging for your business, but you didn't ask for a read back, you can still go to the journalist and say, 'That's not what I said. As you're aware, I mentioned x, y, z.' Remember though, they will have recorded the interview to help them with transcription, and to also protect themselves. If, however, you feel that what you said has been taken out of context and twisted to meet their agenda, you do have some opportunity for redress. If you feel really aggrieved and this could affect your reputation, you can go to the journalist and say, 'I'm not happy that this has happened. And I would like my quotes to be changed.'

If the story stays the same, and you're still unhappy about it, you can go down the road of complaining to the Press Complaints Commission (PCC). But only do this in extreme cases, and make sure that you have sought advice from someone who is a specialist in crisis communications working in PR, so they can look at all the facts, and how everything is portrayed. If you can solve any disputes amicably, it is always best to do so. One area that is always a bone of contention for business owners is headlines. Headlines encourage readers to click on a story or read more. They appeal to people on a much bigger scale but in some instances, to get that readability, things might be changed to make a story look more appealing.

I've had several instances when clients have come to me, really upset, saying, 'The headline is wrong. What can I do?' In extreme cases, I've been able to get them changed along with other more inaccurate elements of the story as it's been a sensitive subject matter. It may well be that if I've been helping the client with the piece in the first place, we will have previously agreed with the journalist how that story will be reflected in the publication. But because I will have this in writing, I can then respond to the journalist, asking for changes to be made as we'd agreed to a, b, c and not x, y, and z.

This chapter is not in this book to scare you. It's to make you aware of the importance of preparation. You need to know exactly what you want out of any interview. You need to know what you're going to say with those pre-prepared key messages, so you always look at things in a more positive light. Do not go into any interview saying something negative about someone else, because it's likely that you're going to become the story. It's then something that can enable the story to run and run, especially when you're talking about national media.

Things can get changed. Apologies can be made in print or online or in some cases, in broadcast too. Sometimes, it just takes a bit of time, and it's much better that those stories haven't run in the first place. So, really safeguard yourself as much as you possibly can, and you will still be able to effectively make the most of the power of PR.

9

MAKING A CAMPAIGN SUCCESSFUL

There may come a time when you want to explore bringing out a news story or a campaign that you can use to raise awareness about a cause or something that you're passionate about. It could well be that there's something in your story that lends itself to more of a campaigning element. If this is the case, you need to think strategically about how to make that as successful as possible.

WHAT WORKS AND WHY

Often you can see that the most successful news stories have a news hook, which means they have a reason to run when they do, whether that's an awareness day, an awareness month or an awareness week, or there's something tied to a specific time as to why the media should be featuring your story right now.

For instance, you will know from reading this book that I'm a huge fan of all forms of storytelling and it should come as no surprise that I think books are a brilliant way for you to tell your story and share your expertise on a much wider scale. Writing a book is a brilliant introductory point for anyone who is looking to find out more about you. Once they have read it, they will see what an expert you are in your field and will then want to find out how to work with you, so you can take them up to the next rung of your value ladder with a new offering. Aside from anything else, it's a great opportunity to introduce people to your world and what you do as a business owner, so they can continue working with you on a much larger scale. This works particularly well if you're an entrepreneur.

But when it comes to an idea for a campaign, it's always worth sitting down and looking at what's previously been in the media and the kind of things that do and don't work.

* * *

PR Case study

In November 2019, I was approached by a lovely lady who wanted to work with me as she had an idea for a campaign where she could introduce an hour's free childcare for any mums who needed to have time out to have a smear test. When she came to me, she said she was planning to do it, and should she do it straight away? Instead, I suggested I would go away and see if there was a timelier reason for her to run her campaign in the imminent future so we could maximise what she was planning to do. It turned out that cervical cancer prevention week ran in January. So, instead of just ploughing ahead in November, we maximised her exposure and the story, so that it ran at the start of 2020.

As she had come to me in time, I was able to write the release, gather any images from her and had time to highlight what she was doing in advance to the media. It meant that, rather than her just doing a one-off event and journalists saying, 'Nice idea but why should we run this now?' we were able to maximise the impact she had on the women she was trying to help and were still able to highlight her business at the same time.

In the end, she was featured in a big feature on *Mail Online, independent.co.uk*, and in lots of regional and local media, including *Families online, Emma's Diary*, Essex TV, and *The Ilford Recorder* (which was key for local recognition of her business). By the time we finished the campaign, which we worked together on for a month, she was featured in seven different publications. In terms of raising her profile, it was huge. But it was the careful handling of what it was that she wanted to say and her sharing of her story on *Mail Online* that catapulted awareness around what it was that she was doing.

Thinking strategically about how you can reach your business and PR goals in conjunction with each other is so important. In the example of the UK's first drive-in wedding, for instance, it worked because at the time, apart from it being a UK first, it also highlighted a solution for so many couples who were struggling with only having fifteen relatives being present at their weddings. It was also different and unique, plus we had great pictures and video to accompany the story.

Uplifting stories that highlight how someone has gone from a certain point to where they are now, featuring their journeys, also work well. They could be features for publications such as "Bossing It" in *The Sun* and for the *Femail* section of *Mail Online*, or the weekly big four magazines of *Woman, Woman's Own, Best* and *Bella*. Then also for the Thursday women's magazines such as *Take a Break, That's Life! Real People*, and *Chat* magazines.

What works with many of the stories they feature is that there's usually a wider hook. I was approached by a client who came to me recently saying, "I think I've got a story, but I'm not sure. And I really want to focus on getting myself out there, but I think I'm just too close to everything to know whether it will be of interest to a journalist." We sat down and completed a ninety-minute PR Strategy Session together, where I asked her a series of questions and was able to effectively unpick her story.

At the end of a session, I go away and write up each client's story and provide them with their all-important key messages and some feature ideas. By the end of this session, I already knew she had a brilliant story that would be perfect with a festive news hook. In this instance, before I'd even written up the story, I approached one of the four big women's weekly magazines, and although they were already full for most of their Christmas content, because it was such a strong story, they made space for this interview to happen.

It's worth knowing that journalists love exclusives and being able to have the first run of an exclusive story. It's well worth bearing this in mind when you want a story to run. If you're releasing a big campaign, as you would do if you were a bigger brand, then you would look to release that across the board, and a great starting point for this is getting The Press Association or PA Media on board as well as any other news related wires, because they can help you have a far bigger reach. But when it comes to putting your business out there and telling your story, especially if there's a campaigning element, it's well worth looking at giving your story to one publication as an exclusive.

* * *

PR case study

Independent Road Safety Campaigner, Meera Naran

In October 2020, I began working with the incredibly inspirational Meera Naran. When she came to me, she said, 'I've spoken to three or four other different PR agencies, but no one wants to take this any further and I don't understand why.' And the honest answer was, I didn't understand why either. Up until that point, Meera had appeared in most mainstream media. Throughout 2019, after losing her eight-year-old son Dev in a traffic collision on a stretch of smart motorway, she'd been featured on *Panorama*, *BBC Breakfast*, ITV's *This Morning* and featured in most national newspapers. I think, on first sight, those other PR agencies and practitioners had looked at the swathe of coverage and thought there was nothing else they could do for her. But this is where they had underestimated the power of strategic PR storytelling.

In this instance, each agency had considered PR only in terms of media relations and securing coverage. It's easy to forget that it's part of a way to be able to secure visibility, and storytelling is an incredibly powerful tool to enable you to be able to get your campaign more exposure, and to drive things forward. Working alongside Meera has meant that I've been able to guide her in terms of any messaging for interviews that we have agreed will be good exposure for her. It's meant that we have steered her campaign to where it is today. In June 2021, she was awarded an MBE, which was such a brilliant recognition of all the work she's doing in terms of safer drivers on safer roads. Her campaign is ongoing and will continue. There is so much I could say about her in terms of what an incredible lady she is, and how she is selflessly using her grief to help others and provide hope.

What those other PR practitioners failed to recognise when they were approached by Meera was how impactful her campaign could be, and how much it could help save lives. Because through harnessing an experience, or something that has happened to you, which has formed an enormous part of your story, you really can go on and impact the lives of others on a much greater scale. And this is exactly what Meera has done. When she first came to me, she was speaking to any media that approached her. Instead, now we look at which opportunities work for her. We began with a larger interview in *The Sunday Times* that firmly put her on the map in terms of pushing for answers around smart motorways. What followed saw her begin working as an independent road safety campaigner in parallel with both National Highways and the Department of Transport to effect real change. It's meant she's been able to support recent education campaigns for drivers, been able to see through the changes she'd suggested as part of the government's eighteen-point Action Plan, including getting changes made to the Highway Code. And using her strong research and analytical skills, she has not only suggested what improvements could be made, but the best ways for them to be implemented. Campaigning in Dev's memory, she has opened people's eyes to the way that things can be done, providing hope to so many others who otherwise might not have had it.

Meera Naran - (www.meeranaran.com)

* * *

If you're passionate about a campaign, or there's an issue that stems from a moment that has changed everything for you, PR is a brilliant way to help you amplify it. But please do it strategically and do it with the understanding of the impact that you can have on the lives of others as you go forward, as this will help you maximise your chances of success. When it comes to making your campaign successful, ensure you have a kit of parts that will work for all the media. This includes professional images, knowing the angles for your story, those key messages for when you do any interviews. It also includes you knowing what you want the outcome for any media interview to be. Video will also maximise your chances of success. And if you're releasing new news, a well-written press release tied to a specific date or calendar moment, such as an awareness day or Mother's Day for instance, will be invaluable.

PRESS RELEASES

I should mention press releases here as I'm aware that I haven't said anything about them elsewhere in this book. It's not that I don't use them, it's just they have their own place. If you're releasing new news about a book or something that you're launching like a campaign or charity foundation, a press release is absolutely the right thing to have. If you're also releasing a news story, again a press release is invaluable. Local and regional media like them for award wins and book releases as they can, if they're well-written, pick them up and run the contents of them verbatim online or in their local publication. But overall, if you're looking to get yourself or your business mentioned, unless you're specifically announcing anything new, you don't need to write one, so save yourself the time and effort. And if you don't know how to write one, please get a professional to do it for you.

Here are some tips about writing one:

- Always think about a headline that will be interesting to a journalist
- Your top paragraph should answer the all-important five w's i.e, Who, What, Where Why and When
- Keep your language simple and concise – write as if you are explaining something to a friend in the pub always thinking about the publication you are writing for
- Include a date and if it's to be sent out straight away, make sure you say **for immediate release**
- Always include contact details of where you can be found. An email and telephone number are best
- Include a Notes to Editors section at the bottom, which includes details about your company. This is known as a boiler plate and having one of these already pre-written is always useful
- Try to not add in any information that's unnecessary. Seven paragraphs are a good amount of text
- Include a quote from yourself as the business owner, stating your position in the company i.e., Founder

PR case study

Eloho Efemuai

The talented Eloho Efemuai came to me in 2019 and we completed a PR Strategy Session together. At this time, Eloho said, 'I have so much going on but I don't actually know what should be in my story and what shouldn't.' This can be the problem for many small business owners, knowing what you need to focus on to ensure your core messaging comes across.

Eloho is a professional singer and organises huge charity fundraising events that include flying people from all over the world into Scotland to complete gospel events near her home-town. But she's also a successful Social Media Manager and is helping women feel empowered through getting clear on their messaging to grow and scale their ventures and businesses. As we went through the session, it dawned on me that everything that Eloho does is about communication and communicating with others. Whether it's through music, events, or social media, she's showing her clients how to harness social media for good.

About two minutes from the end of the session, she said to me, 'Oh and there's this radio station called Heart Song Live, and I broadcast four mornings a week and I've converted my garage into a professional radio studio.' As I started my journalism career in radio, my ears pricked up. It turns out that Eloho broadcasts positive messages to people in Edinburgh and beyond so they can start their days in the right way. Bearing in mind this is two minutes before we end the session, I knew right then and there that this was her story. It was the hook that would help her secure media coverage about everything else she did. When I asked her how many listeners she had, at the time she had 10,000 a month. Now she has more than 14,000 listeners a month and Heart Song Live is Edinburgh's leading digital radio station. When I told her this was her story, she looked a bit confused, but then when she first approached me for her session, she had already told me that she didn't think PR would work for her. She'd tried it before and had spent a lot of money trying to secure coverage with not much in the way of a return. So, I asked if anyone had sat down with her and gone through her story in the way I had just done, and the response was no.

In fairness, it's a common mistake I see all the time from other PR agencies. I always remember working and being given new clients in PR and being told, 'There you go. This is a new client – now get them coverage,' and all I knew was a few details about them. We never had time to sit down with them for an hour and a half. That may well have happened with more senior members of staff, but I was the one expected to secure the coverage and yet, knowing what I do now, I was only armed with half of the story. Until you find out what the story is, and until you understand what the angles are, you can't tell what journalists will be interested in and you can't hope to secure effective PR that draws on storytelling in an exceptional way.

After Eloho told me her story, I approached a trusted journalist contact in Scotland, and not long afterwards, Eloho had a full-page magazine feature about her and her radio station from her converted garage at her home in Edinburgh. I also approached *The Daily Record*, which is Scotland's leading national newspaper. This is a big learning in terms of how to maximise your chances of success. They loved Eloho's story. They sent a journalist out to interview her and a photographer to take bespoke images. But then the feature didn't run, despite much chasing on my part.

A few months later. Eloho contacted me saying, 'Nicola, I'm going to be in *Come Dine with Me* on Channel Four. Is there anything you can do to help me in terms of PR?' Having worked in TV publicity for several years, I didn't want to stand on Channel 4's toes, so I said to her, 'If the channel doesn't contact you and you still haven't heard anything from them until a few days before the transmission date, come back to me.' A few days before the programme was broadcast, she did just that. The Channel 4 press office hadn't been in touch. So, I contacted the journalist at *The Daily Record* who I'd originally spoken to, and said, 'Do you remember that story with Eloho and the radio station? It hasn't run and I think it's because you didn't have enough of a hook, but now she's going to be on *Come Dine with Me*, and so here's your hook!'

They spoke to Eloho again as a top-up chat to the interview she had already completed, captured a screen grab of the TV show, and on the Monday, when Eloho's *Come Dine with Me* episode was shown, they ran a double page spread about Eloho, her radio station, how she was a social media manager empowering and inspiring women to be the best version of themselves, both in print and online. That's why it's so important to follow up with journalists and ensure you have a hook, especially if something hasn't previously run. This is how you can maximise your chances of success, with a time specific angle.

Eloho Efemuai – (www.elohoefemuai.co.uk)

* * *

If you have had a traumatic upbringing, you might want to do something around Mother's Day, or if you have lost your mum, and you want it to run around Mother's Day, then think about that as an angle. You need to always think, 'Why would the media be interested in this story?' and then never, ever give up. When you're approaching the media but don't have everything fully aligned, as in Eloho's case, the guidance and expertise I was able to give her meant she secured PR that she'd never thought was possible. It may well be that sometimes, you will approach the media, and you will have a hook, and they will still say it just doesn't quite work for them. Perhaps they have already gathered enough pieces around International Women's Day or whatever your hook is, but further down the line, there will usually be something else that will work.

* * *

PR case study

Claire Sweet

Another great example of making a campaign work for you and being able to tell your story is a client I worked with at the beginning of launching NJRPR. Claire Sweet is a Financial Adviser and was looking to position herself as a money coach. Again, we had a PR Strategy Session, so I could unpick and write her story. We worked out that her story centred around the fact that she had a field of alpacas at the bottom of her garden and she's able to see 'her boys' from her home office where she offers financial advice. Why is this juxtaposition great in media terms? How many money coaches do you know that own a herd of alpacas?

A few years ago, Claire trekked the Inca Trail in Peru, raising money for the Kent Air Ambulance. But whilst on that trek, she fell in love with alpacas, the woolly creatures that are well known to inhabit Macchu Picchu. As a result of this new-found love, she made it her dream to one day have a property big enough so she could have a field at the bottom of her garden, where the alpacas would be able to roam. Bearing in mind that Alpacas take up quite a lot of space, so she needed a big field.

Because she is financially astute, and does what she does, Claire proved that what had at first seemed impossible, was, in fact, possible. Through managing their finances, she and her husband, Phil, were able to move to a bigger property. As a result, Claire came to me and was about to take ownership of her first five alpacas. The problem was, she didn't have any pictures. So, once her boys were settled, I travelled with a news photographer to see Claire and the alpacas and after a couple of hours, we managed to get the alpacas all vaguely looking in the right direction. And with those pictures, we were then able to use them for securing PR opportunities.

Claire's story first appeared in the business section of the *Mirror.co.uk*. In it, she also spoke about another story from when Claire had been a student and had just two pounds fifty to her name in supermarket vouchers that she had to live off for an entire week. The more worrying thing for Claire was she didn't feel that she could tell anyone else she was in this predicament and as it was, she also felt trapped in a relationship that she didn't want to be in. She realised in that moment, she was never going to rely on anyone else again when it came to her money, and she was going to always oversee things, financially speaking. And that is why she became a money coach, specialising in helping women. It's something she's hugely passionate about and feels that no woman should ever have to feel trapped in a relationship, abusive or otherwise, by their finances.

After being in the *Mirror.co.uk*, I secured Claire an opportunity to be on a podcast, which meant that she had to travel into London to record it. Initially she really didn't want to, but I persuaded her otherwise, as it was for *About Time Magazine*. As a result of doing that interview, not only did she end up with a new client, as one of the people that was also taking part in the podcast liked her, but she was invited to speak on at least two different stages, in front of hundreds of women. It was a pivotal turning point for her business. I then secured Claire and her alpacas a double page spread in *The Telegraph Magazine*. She was featured giving her expert comments in *Stylist* and numerous other publications, including *Health and Wellbeing* and *Moneywise*. Then a few months later, she was featured in *The Guardian*, in a double page spread. Again, Claire living her dream life, alongside her alpacas.

Peace Together Money Coaching with Claire Sweet (www.-peacetogether.co.uk)

* * *

If you have a story and a strong enough news hook, these are all things that will maximise your chances of success. But as you saw from the example of the UK's first drive-in wedding, it is very much about ensuring that the story is sold to the journalist in the correct way. That story could have completely gone under the radar and not been run at all. As it was, it went viral in the UK and internationally, and has since been shortlisted for and won awards.

But in all the above case studies, these stories needed additional guidance from myself to help them maximise their success. So, if you have a campaign or you have something that you really want to make more noise about and you're doing it to help others, I would advise you to get professional help from someone like myself who works in PR, who helps people with cause-led campaigns and who can help you understand not only your story, but the media landscape, so you can reach and impact as many people with your message as possible.

PR is an incredible tool to be able to help you reach more people to make them aware of the changes you are looking to make to help others. I think it's one of the most special things you can do as an entrepreneur and business owner, to look to help change people's lives, or make a difference to others in a quite unique and special way. But make sure you have the right support behind you, to make this a reality.

10

NOW WHAT?

Securing media coverage can be the most exciting thing. But getting truly visible doesn't just stop with one piece of PR. The more that you are seen, quoted, and identified as being an expert in your chosen field, the better. But once the initial euphoria of landing some media coverage wears off, you can be left wondering 'what next?' And indeed, I often get messages saying, 'Well, I've been featured in this publication, but nothing has happened.' You must remember this is just the start of your journey. Your ideal clients aren't going to come knocking on your door because they have seen you somewhere once. Over an eleven-hour period they need to see you up to six times. That can be on social media, through a piece of PR, a Facebook live, a couple of Instagram stories. Consistency is key to everything and as I've mentioned earlier, you can't rely on PR in isolation to get you noticed. It should only ever be part of your marketing. When people come to me and say, 'I haven't heard anything because of that piece of PR, so it's clearly not working,' my question is always the same:

What did you do to maximise the PR that you secured?

Nine times out of ten, there is usually complete silence or a half-hearted, 'Well, I shared it on my Facebook page,' response. But it's not enough and it's not the way to maximise PR coverage. Planning is everything when it comes to communications, and this includes once you have secured some publicity for yourself or your business. The question you need to ask yourself is, 'How can I secure further brand awareness and leads using social media?'

Once you have been featured in any publication, whether that's talking on your local BBC radio station, being featured on the national news, being quoted in national newspapers or in magazines, or as a guest interviewee on a podcast that's big in your industry, you need to tell people this has happened. The best way to start doing this is on the home page of your website. Right at the top, directly underneath your picture, you need to have an "As featured in…" followed by the logos of each of the media outlets where you have been quoted or seen. These logos are highlighting how you have provided expert commentary or tips, or your story has been featured in these publications. Remember, it's never a given that you can secure any editorial. That's why earned media is so infinitely valuable.

Unless someone asks for them, you also don't need to provide the actual links to the pieces. But it's important that you don't shy away from highlighting where you have been featured. I had a client that I worked with for quite a while. I remember looking at her website, and she had all of the media logos buried at the bottom of the home page. In short, they had been buried, along with that recognition you get when people see that you have been featured in some top media titles. She must have had at least fifteen logos of top tier magazines and newspapers – and not one of them could easily be seen.

Think of it like this. If someone clicks onto a website and can easily see from the homepage that you have been featured in *The Guardian*, *The Telegraph Magazine* and *Stylist*, how do you think they will view you? It makes them think, 'Hang on a moment, this is someone I need to find out more about. *Stylist* is one of my favourite publications.'

It really does have that effect. I always remember back in 2010 I was looking to book a mind reader for part of the evening entertainment for our wedding. I didn't know where to start, so I typed in mind reader. This is the kind of thing which will be happening all the time as potential clients of yours try to solve their pain point, especially if they haven't come across you yet. I visited a chap's website, and it had lots of media logos such as *OK!* magazine and *The Sun* and it also said, 'as recommended by Simon Cowell'. I didn't go any further. I picked up the phone and called him, reasoning, well, if he's been featured in all these magazines and he's also recommended by Simon Cowell, that's good enough for us.

Now, perhaps I should have done my due diligence a bit better than that, however, in fairness, he was brilliant at what he did. He came along on the night for our wedding, and everyone loved him. So, it worked for him because he ended up with a last-minute, profitable wedding booking in November, which was out of season as it was on a Sunday too. And that is how it works. The power of someone needing something from you. They book in to work with you because apart from anything else, your message resonates with them, they have read your story somewhere, or come across an expert comment that you have made, and they realise they need someone that can help them with their time-blocking or business strategy.

Your ideal client is sitting out there somewhere, doing some research on Google for the service or product that you provide. Are you the person who can help them sort their finances once and for all? Are you the person who can provide them with a thoughtful gift for a loved one? Are you the one who can help them organise a big event? And from that point onwards, they find your website (which you should always think of as your shop front, highlighting the current thing that you're working on), they see you're an expert in your field, and they start to follow you, wanting to find out more.

For instance, when it comes to me highlighting this book, front and centre on my website should be *The Power of PR* book, now available on my www.njrpr.com website. Because that's what I want to tell people I have to offer right now – followed by the chance to join my four-day 'From Incognito to Interviewed' challenge that I'm running on Facebook.

The next thing you should do with any piece of PR is make sure you're telling people, not just once but several times over on social media. Not in a 'look at me' kind of a way, but in an 'I've written this piece and I'd love to hear what your greatest take-away is,' way, adding value perspective. And of course, if the piece is from an online site, you can then share the link directly, as that's the actual link to the coverage.

You can also ask your audience what they think of it and what other topics they would like to see you talking about. It's about driving engagement and interest and maximising the PR opportunity that you have just secured. Remember, with all these things, the more engagement you get, the more likes you get, the more comments you get, the better the algorithms will work in your favour, and it will get shared more widely with more people.

Equally, make sure that you email your list and provide them with the link to the piece where you have been featured so they can go away and read it for themselves. Again, your email list should consist of your ideal clients. Up until this point, they may have just been watching in the background and observing quietly. I still get messages from people after they see a post saying, 'I've been watching you for a while now.' And it's true – people like to feel like they know you, that they're getting to understand who you are and what you do, and why they should work with you as opposed to someone else in your industry. The thing to remember with any competitors is that there are always enough clients to go around. Whilst it's good to keep an eye on what they're doing, I always advocate staying in your own lane rather than going down the road of comparisonitis.

In August 2021, I went to a book launch in central London. In fairness, I was there just to support the host. I walked in and just said hello. I didn't think that I knew anyone apart from her. But women were coming up to me saying, 'You're Nicola, aren't you?' and 'Hello, Nicola, how are you?' I wasn't entirely sure who everyone was, but because my business and my presence are online, and people know me as 'the PR lady who specialises in storytelling,' they felt that they already knew me. There were lots of comments such as, 'I've been following you for ages' or 'I've heard about you and your PR membership.' This, for me, is the power of making sure that your messaging is consistent, that you stay in your own lane, and don't worry about being compared to others in your industry - literally just do your own thing and make sure that people understand what it is that you stand for.

That brings me on to how you maximise your media presence, because I think that when it comes to media, as much as we've talked about the fact that your PR strategy should be very much aligned with your business objectives, as you would in your business, you aren't going to be selling twenty-four hours a day, seven days a week. There are going to be peaks and troughs where you're going to be doing things in your business. This is why your PR strategy and objectives have to be the same. You don't want to just be 'on' all the time. You want to be looking at times when you want that additional powerful boost of exposure that only PR can give, but you also need to balance it out with providing value to your audience, so they have a reason to continue following you. When you are looking for more impact to be made, this is when your story and storytelling can come into their own and, as we've discussed, can go on to impact other people's lives. Coupled with finding that news hook or reason for your story to be run at that given moment in time, this is how your media presence can skyrocket.

Google you...

Do me a favour and take a short break away from reading this book and type your name into Google. What comes up? The number one thing that should always come up is your website. But if you're managing to have a good media presence, you will see the links to lots of media outlets featured underneath. Now, the media outlets to be on are the ones that are very clever with SEO (Search Engine Optimisation). It means the sites that are higher up the Google search ranks and so show up first and foremost. Those are the ones that you want to be featured in. For Lisa Johnson (who we met earlier in this book), if you type in her name, you not only get her website, but you also get the feature in *Metro*, which talks about how she went from being thirty thousand pounds in debt to becoming a millionaire within four years. That was a piece that I secured for Lisa as part of her being in my VIP level of my PR Mastery Membership. It ran as a full-page piece in print and online in January 2021. It was then picked up by *The Sun* online, and then *Mail Online*, who asked permission if they could use pictures from her Instagram feed. She ended up with five hundred new Instagram followers and because of that one piece, she now has three big, and very SEO friendly features that are highlighted under her name.

If you remember about DA scores, they are all sites that have a DA of 89+ - in other words, they're huge. You have to remember that those new followers could easily turn into potential clients. It was a brilliant way for her to be able to get leads. Her media presence, when you look online, even on the first two pages of Google, contain many of the pieces that I've secured for her, because I've strategically looked at the places which will give her the best SEO. Yes, there's a feature on there from *Female First*. Some people might think well, why would ask would you want to be in *Female First*? Because their SEO is brilliant, and their SEO means you will be found by the people who need you most. Talking of pieces in the media, when it came to me approaching *TALK Radio* for Lisa to be a guest on *Badass Woman's Hour*, they asked me to send the links to some of the media coverage she already had. They were, in effect, gauging whether she would be a big enough guest and of course, she absolutely was. She had a half an hour interview with Harriet Minter all about her story and how she helps others through the work she does as a business strategist. On national radio, with millions of listeners in a prime show that attracts a predominantly female audience.

Strategically, this was lined up to run just ahead of Lisa's challenge for her One to Many course. That is how you increase your media presence, thinking strategically about how one piece could feed into others, and making sure that the places that you're targeting work well for SEO.

There is nothing more important than taking your audience with you on your journey. Apart from anything else, you will end up with an incredibly loyal audience as a result. And a loyal audience is worth everything. They're the people that are going to shout about any of your wins. They're the ones that are going to help you get ahead when you have something to tell them about. And yes, they're also the ones that are going to support you in any launch that you may do. This all might work best for online businesses but there's no reason why, as a bricks and mortar business, you can't help your audience in this way too.

Another way to maximise any PR is to email your list and mention it to them. This is a list of people who have subscribed to find out what you have to offer and have agreed that they would like to hear from you on a more regular basis. Through emailing them regularly, this allows them to get to know you, your personality, and parts of your story because yes, yet again, this is how you should also be sharing any media and PR pieces. You can let your audience know things about you, things that will help them resonate with you. Don't forget that people buy from people. Be honest. The most successful business owners I know are the ones who just tell it as it is.

Quite often on my lives in my membership, I'll tell them about Rufus, our cockerpoo puppy and what he's been up to, or the fact that we were looking to sell our house and the massive saga that followed as a result. Allow them to get to know you as a person, as much as anything else. They remain loyal to you so, let them into your world. It doesn't mean to say you have to tell them everything, warts, and all. As with any pieces of PR, you share with them the parts of your story that you're happy to share. And when things go wrong? Admit that it didn't go quite according to plan and hold your hands up. We're all human, after all, and no one gets everything right all the time.

Even if you run a bricks and mortar business, if you wish to continue to have success in the business world, you will have seen from the pandemic, it's now vital to have an online element to your business. No one could have foreseen how everything would shut down in the way that it did, but the ones that benefitted were the businesses that were already online. There are going to be so many more people that don't want to return to their current jobs, or they're doing it for the time being, but they now have half an eye on the fact they really have a passion for something else and want to become their own bosses and have the flexibility to do things their own way. They want to understand how to be able to build a successful business online, and how to market it effectively. And I'd argue that you can't market things effectively unless you use PR.

Yes, PR is very much part of the marketing mix, but it's incredibly powerful because it allows you to connect with people. And whilst connection is important, impacting the lives of others to help them, is everything. PR should not just be seen as an awareness-raising tool, to enhance your ego. PR should be seen as a force for good. It should be seen as a way to reach people that really need help. It's a way to solve people's problems. But unless people know that you exist, they can't find you and they can't come to you.

So, take your audience on a journey with you. Tell them when you have been featured and where. Tell them what it was like for you when you were interviewed. Were you scared? Were you nervous? Were you excited? How did it go? I remember telling my audience all about the time I received a message on Twitter from ITV News, and it was a week before I launched my last children's book, *Mug the Wumph the Dancing Wizard*, dedicated to my late dad. The message was as follows, 'Nicola, we're looking for a children's author just like you because JK Rowling's brought out her *Ickabog* book, and we'd like to speak to you. Any chance we can?' I went back, straight away, saying yes, I'd love to help and what did they need from me. Within half an hour, a camera operator and producer were in my back garden, ready to film for the ITV evening news. In that half an hour, as I told my audience, I had been living in complete chaos. So, I cleared my entire spare room from all the junk and made it all look good for filming. I also made sure I had copies of my book to hand, and I was wearing a dress that was the right colour for the book. I had also checked that I looked how I wanted to look on camera.

As part of the piece, they said to me, 'Right, we don't have long because we're going to turn this around for the evening news.' My response? 'Would it work better for you if I talk in sound-bites to make it easier for the team back in London to edit the report?' The producer looked at the camera operator and he looked at the producer, and then they both nodded enthusiastically and said yes please. So, I found out where they wanted me in the news package and what ideally, they wanted me to say, and then I made it all fit together.

But before the camera started filming, I also asked if it would be ok if when they came to me for my cutaway (when they have to introduce you in the piece and say what you do) that I would be reading my new children's book that was about to be published. They agreed and so that's what I did. And I was featured on the

ITV evening news as a children's author. My name popped up on screen and everyone in my audience became as excited as I was and, because it was just a week before my book launch, it really helped in terms of raising awareness about my new book and how I hoped it helped the children who weren't at school at that time to be able to go on a magical adventure, as they were already missing out on so much.

Did I mention it just once on Facebook?

No, I told every single person I could think of about it and what had happened and how exciting it was, a week before my book launch, and did they want to join me for the launch as I'd love their support if they did. I also completed lives, added it to my stories and was messaging people for the rest of the night and well into the next day. And I told them about the room, and the mess I now had to clear from our main bedroom but how it had been a great wake up call to declutter the house. I can't stress how important it is that you let people get to know you. It's so important and it's how you get a loyal audience. The more you tell them - the good and the bad – the more they will trust and follow what you're up to. Talk, engage, share, and always bring them along with you. There's no reason you can't do that for every single piece of media that you secure. You can tell them how you hadn't previously considered doing something like this, but this opportunity arose, and isn't it a great idea because you can now share it with them.

I have tokophobia, which is an extreme fear of giving birth. So having J was a huge deal for me, which involved a psychological assessment and many more hospital appointments than usual.

But alongside that fear, I also knew that I had so much love to give a child, that it was worth all the anguish, anxiety, and stress that would come from me having to give birth. But it's important that you tell people about these things, as it's important they can put themselves in your shoes. Perhaps they too have a deep-rooted fear, but seeing you openly talk about it and how you overcame it through love means they feel braver and that they too can do something they previously thought was impossible.

When I had Covid in March 2020, right at the beginning of the pandemic, I wrote an opinion piece in *The Daily Telegraph* that appeared not only in print, but also online. It was later picked up by both LBC and BBC Radio Five Live. As a result of doing those two interviews, I was also able to mention my previous book. And I was also able to talk about what else was going on and how we needed to not only focus on our own health and well-being, but we also needed to be able to think about the children who were not around their friends, and that was why I brought out the publication of my new children's book earlier than planned. Hopefully, you can start to see how you can make everything work for you, as well as being able to make it work for others too.

You just have to think strategically and work out how your audience wants to hear from you. Storytelling in this way is by far the best way to engage people and to encourage them to get to know you so they can see who you are, what matters most to you and to work out if your values align.

Integrating any PR and media success with a social media strategy really is the key to success. It used to be that someone only needed to see your business seven times before they joined your audience or bought from you. With so much noise, choice and messaging available, thanks to social channels, this has changed. People now need to see you at least three times this number to cut through. I want you to think about the last time you went to a dinner party. What was the one thing that stayed with you long after the evening? The stories you heard and the emotion they evoked. It's the same for your audience; stories, especially your story, help you to create meaningful connections and once that happens, it will enable you to help them as only you can.

IN CONCLUSION...

P R is not ER, but I get how it can feel scary. Hopefully now you have read this book, you will now feel more confident to take that next step to get visible.

Throughout these pages, there have been examples of businesses and individuals who have maximised PR. And there have been examples of entrepreneurs who, despite facing so many obstacles, have shown their audience how they overcame them and used those moments to be able to tell their stories more effectively. As a result, they have reached and impacted other people's lives through doing what they do, whether, like Lisa Johnson, they're a business strategist who has helped thousands of people learn how to do online courses and memberships, whether they're a money coach like Claire Sweet, who has been able to show people how it's possible to have a dream and how they can make it happen through budgeting, or whether it's an incredible high-end events organiser like Saheli Mirpuri, who had the spark of an idea, made it a reality and was wondering whether it could help others in the wedding industry feel empowered at a difficult time. Hopefully, you can see through each example how they have harnessed the power of PR to be able to touch other people's lives.

Just as Meera Naran has with her incredible on-going campaign for road safety and safer drivers on safer roads. She is completely inspirational and making the world of difference to others, in memory of her son Dev.

More and more, I'm so fortunate to be working with other female entrepreneurs who want to make a real difference. Those are the ones that really want to get out there:

Lawyer Joanne Fisher. She wants to get it written into law that after having a baby, there should be a six-month leeway when no one can approach a woman about her being in debt. I know from my own perspective maternal mental health is a real issue. And through doing what she's doing, Joanne is highlighting this important issue and trying to make a change, to help others further down the line, so they don't have to go through what she also went through.

(www.joannefisherlaw.co.uk)

Tanya Ibberson, another client who despite being a qualified accountant found herself in huge amounts of debt because of a previous abusive relationship. She is now ensuring that other businesswomen are aware of how to not only manage their debt, but how to maximise their assets.

(www.financialwingwoman.com)

Antoinette Daniel is paving the way for change in the cleaning industry with her ethical business, Just Helpers, turning over a million pounds a year but ensuring that everyone on her team gets paid above the minimum wage. Through securing PR in *Metro*, *Good Housekeeping*, *Fabulous* magazine, and many more titles besides, she's trying to shine a light on the fact that cleaners need to be valued too.

(www.justhelpers.co.uk)

Camille Plews is showing other business owners how they can get more leads into their business and therefore make themselves a success. But she's a mum running a successful company from the caravan on her driveway at home, and she's inspiring people through doing that. I don't know about you, but I like to work from the car from time to time, just so that I can have some headspace, so I completely get the need for Camille's caravan.

(www.camilleplews.com)

A very wise mentor once told me, it's PR, not ER. It means that when you're in the thick of a PR campaign, or things feel like they're not going right, or you're dealing with a crisis, or something's happening, it can feel like it's the worst thing in the world. And I get that. When you first go out there and decide you're going to start securing PR, it can feel scary.

Remember, I've been there too. Back in 2016, I had to put myself out there to get my first children's book out there, otherwise, no one would have known about *James and the Amazing Gift*. That led to the opportunity for the lovely Dr Ranj from TV narrating the second book in the series, *James and the Birthday Balloon*.

But hopefully, through following all the steps in this book, you will see that PR doesn't have to be baffling, complicated, or scary, and by taking it one step at a time, you will feel more confident about putting yourself out there. You now know the things that you need in place before you even go out there to get PR. Remember, it's all about knowing your story. Having those professional pictures, having a short and a long biography already written, and a website.

Once you have these and are clear on your messaging and what you want the outcome for any interview to be, you're all set. Don't forget, your website doesn't have to be all singing, all dancing; it can be just a simple landing page.

At the end of the day, the media just want to have something that they can point people to. And at the end of the day, you just want to be able to tell people how you can help them. If you're planning to launch a course or a membership, or if you're planning to unveil a new product, use your website to let people know about those things. But get the website URL featured in any PR that you secure. If you have a product that you want to talk about, again it should be front and centre on your website so you can get it featured in 'Stylist Loves' and pieces like that. But alongside it, don't forget to also tell your story.

Hopefully, now you will realise that it's a mistake to approach a journalist and ask them to run great big pieces around your course or membership, as they won't be interested. They're interested in you but dig deep. Don't just think it's some on-the-surface thing. It's always so much more. It's the person that has overcome something which could look, from the outside, insurmountable, and yet they have gone on to do incredible things. Think about Meera and her campaign. Think about Lisa. Think about the people that are still campaigning, still trying to make a change to help other people's lives, like Joanne Fisher.

Those are the people who you will feel naturally drawn towards when it comes to do business. The people that have the same values as you. The people who put ethics and integrity above everything else. In short, they care and are heart-led in what they do.

I became a journalist because I love to write. I've always loved storytelling. From being that little six-year-old who wrote her first story about a cat, a witch, and a spaceship, and never wanted to stop writing. That same child at the age of eleven who sat her first English exam at secondary school with the biggest smile on her face, as the paper asked her to write a story. What a gift. Those moments and those feelings have never left me. Every time someone invests in me to help them find and write their stories; I love it more than anything. And it's why I do what I do now, running my own communications agency, specialising in helping entepreneurs like you get visible through strategic PR storytelling.

Having been a journalist for thirteen years, worked in PR for fourteen further years, and this being my fourth book, I think it's fair to say that stories and storytelling are at the heart of who I am. Now it's up to you to harness the power of PR to help you reach your ideal clients so you can effectively grow and scale your business.

Remember, PR is not just an ego-trip or just about awareness raising. It is an incredibly powerful tool when it's used for good.

Make sure you're effectively spreading your message about how you can help others and continue to let them know the transformation or products that you offer. And never give up! Keep going with your media outreach. I know sometimes it can feel like you will never secure anything, but I promise you will, if you just keep going consistently. The more that you do this, the more you will reach those who need you most. This is the true power of PR. And as a by-product of it, you will become known as the expert in your field, increasing your reach and credibility.

But at the heart of it all, you have helped and will continue to help impact other people's lives. And there's nothing more important than that.

IN THEIR OWN WORDS...

"Nicola has helped me get lots of press in the time I've worked with her, and I particularly love that she understands the messaging I want to get out there and finds ways to do just that!"

— LISA JOHNSON, BUSINESS STRATEGIST

"When I approached multiple agents, I honestly had no idea what exactly I was looking for. At the time we were in the middle of the pandemic, I was grieving, looking after my palliative son, my one-year-old daughter, managing work and my campaign needed a lot more focused attention to continue to make positive changes. When I finally met Nicola, I truly believed that Dev had sent her to me to help me cope with everything that was going on and she was exactly the person I needed. Nicola understood my why straight away and since then, has unequivocally supported my how. Campaigning through grief has never been easy and it was always important *for me to separate my personal emotion from campaigning for changes for the greater good. Nicola helped me navigate through this, supporting me to focus on my key points both within my campaign but also in my wider work. She has been there for me on both the good and the not so good days, always pushing me to be better and stay true to my purpose. I will always be truly grateful for her support."*

— MEERA NARAN MBE, INDEPENDENT ROAD SAFETY
CAMPAIGNER

"I've known and worked with Nicola on and off since 2011. She leaves no stone unturned in finding the right, suitable media opportunities and is incredibly knowledgeable when it comes to helping female founders like myself get noticed through PR storytelling."

— TRACY FORSYTH, SUPER COACH, FAST TRACK TO
FEARLESS

"Myself and the team cannot thank you enough!! The coverage and exposure was above and beyond and you have truly been a pleasure to work with! Thank you so so much! I look forward to working with you more in the future and creating more viral weddings!"

— SAHELI MIRPURI, SAHELI EVENTS

"I couldn't be happier with my experience of working with the lovely Nicola. Her knowledge is incredible, and her kind nature has put my mind at ease no-end. Nicola secured lots of beautiful pieces for my book launch and

'held my hand' as I discussed some very sensitive topics. Before meeting Nicola, PR was a rather scary prospect for me, but she has helped me to feel more confident when communicating with and approaching journalists. The articles that have been published have attracted so many new and returning clients and my eyes have well and truly been opened to the power of PR."

— KYLIE ANNA – CONFIDENT MUMS SOCIETY

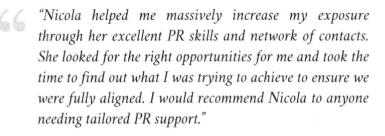

"Nicola helped me massively increase my exposure through her excellent PR skills and network of contacts. She looked for the right opportunities for me and took the time to find out what I was trying to achieve to ensure we were fully aligned. I would recommend Nicola to anyone needing tailored PR support."

— CLAIRE SWEET, PEACE TOGETHER MONEY
COACHING

ABOUT THE AUTHOR

Nicola J Rowley has more than 25+ years' experience in the media, having trained as a journalist and worked nationally and internationally before embarking on a multi-award-winning career in Communications. During this time, she worked both in agency and in-house on some of the UK's most successful PR stunts, campaigns and launches for well-known brands.

In 2019 she launched NJRPR, a Communications Agency helping female entrepreneurs and brands in the entertainment and leisure industries get noticed through strategic PR story-telling.

She was recently Highly Commended in the 2021 national PRCA Awards and was the Silver Award winner in the 2021 CIPR Pride Awards.

instagram.com/nicolajrowleypr

WAYS YOU CAN WORK WITH NICOLA J ROWLEY FROM NJRPR...

PR MASTERY MEMBERSHIP

Results-proven membership where real-time media requests are posted

- Monthly trainings and Journalist Q&A's
- Monthly Picture and Story Clinics
- Weekly lives with Nicola J Rowley

The waitlist can be found here:

https://go.njrpr.com/membership

PR MASTERY – THE COURSE

A nine-week online group program introducing all things PR (a perfect partner to this book)

The waitlist can be found here: https://go.njrpr.com/course

PR STRATEGY SESSIONS

If you're interested in a PR Strategy Session to get clear on your story – email: nicola@njrpr.com for details

1:1 VIP HALF DAYS AND 1:1 VIP FULL DAYS

Contact nicola@njrpr.com to discuss your suitability and needs

SOCIAL MEDIA

Come and say hello in our FREE Facebook group
The Communications Community
https://www.facebook.com/
groups/TheCommunicationsCommunity

Check out our website for the latest on what we're up to:
www.njrpr.com

And don't forget the FREE workbooks to accompany this book
can be found online at:
www.njrpr.com/book

Printed in Great Britain
by Amazon